introduction to INTERPERSONAL COMMUNICATION

introduction to INTERPERSONAL COMMUNICATION

Sara A. Barnhart

THOMAS Y. CROWELL COMPANY
NEW YORK • ESTABLISHED 1834

Published simultaneously in Canada by Fitzhenry & Whiteside, Ltd., Toronto.

Library of Congress Cataloging in Publication Data

Barnhart, Sara A
Introduction to interpersonal communication.
Bibliography: p.
Includes index.
1. Interpersonal communication. 1. Title.
BF637.C45B36 1976 158'.2 75-40140
ISBN 0-690-00855-4

Thomas Y. Crowell Company
666 Fifth Avenue
New York, New York 10019

Typography Design by LIBRA Graphics, Inc.

Manufactured in the United States of America

CONTENTS

PREFACE

The field of Speech Communication is an eclectic one. Originating in the public speaking-debate-oral interpretation tradition, it has more recently been broadened to include material previously associated with such fields as psychology, sociology, anthropology, and linguistics, to name several. We are still in the process of sorting out these matters —a task which, while exciting, is sometimes a bit confusing.

I hope this book will contribute somewhat to that process by ordering the major ideas of interpersonal communication in a fashion comprehensible to the beginning student. Often interpersonal communication books have stayed too close to the pure speech tradition, dealing with areas best suited to public address and persuasion. Or they have gone completely the other direction and thereby lost any particular communication focus. I have tried to avoid both extremes. By using Dean Barnlund's Transactional

Model of Communication throughout, I keep the book's focus always on the *communicative* aspects of the material under discussion.

The two chapters one might least expect to encounter in an introductory book are the second, "Channels of Communication," and the seventh, "Patterns of Communication." Chapter two deals with the human body as a sensory receiver, attempting to explain each of the five senses in such a way as to increase a student's awareness of all the different kinds of potential messages floating around her or him at any moment. This discussion and the frequent descriptions of common everyday experiences are designed to help the students become more aware of their own "sending" and "receiving" communication behavior.

Chapter seven, the final chapter in the book, explores several patterns of communication exchange. The primary purposes of this chapter are, first, to tie together the various aspects of the communication process described in the first six chapters and, second, to reinforce the communicative nature of these aspects. Using a simplified systems theory approach, interpersonal messages—the elements which bind together a communication system—are studied for the effects they have on the system. Both verbal and nonverbal elements of messages exchanged are examined. In every case, however, the focus is on how the people involved in an exchange *perceive* what is occurring.

Throughout, I have attempted to minimize jargon and to avoid, as well, sexist language and examples. Both seem worthwhile goals for a *communication* textbook.

1 WHAT IS COMMUNICATION?

WHY STUDY COMMUNICATION?

"What we have here is a failure to communicate." Why, given the thousands of lines in the hundreds of motion pictures released every year, did this one from *Cool Hand Luke* become such a catch phrase for so many people.

There probably are as many answers to that question as there are people to answer it. For some it may have been a comment on the *quantity* as compared with the *quality* of much communication today between spouses, lovers, ethnic, religious, and sexual groups, political leaders and citizens, teachers and students, and all forms of the mass media and society. For others it may have reflected the cynical nature of some of the current interest in "human relations training," particularly in business, government, and "helping" or correctional institutions. Finally, some may have perceived a gross oversimplification of the problem inherent in the system depicted in the movie. And your own interpretation may be unrelated to any of these.

The above example illustrates one of the basic principles of this book. It is not accurate to think that when we communicate with others, we transfer a precise piece of information from one mind to another. Communication vehicles, like words, signs, movies, do not in and of themselves have meaning, but rather people have meaning for them. The line of dialogue quoted above does not *have* meaning; you apply meaning. Therefore, we can think of communication as a *transaction* in which we and another are attempting to create meaning between us. This does not mean that, if successful, we will always *agree* with one another, but at least we can be more objective and precise about our disagreements.

The idea of creating meaning through communication is not an easy concept to grasp, and we will discuss it in detail later. For now, let us just say that we constantly are trying to understand ourselves and other people and things around us through communication.

Think back over what you did yesterday. Did you talk with anyone? Did you listen to anyone? Did you watch television or listen to music? Did you read a book, newspaper, or magazine? Did you sit somewhere and just watch people or were others watching you? If you did not do *any* of these things, was yesterday a typical day?

Most people spend a great deal of their time communicating in some way with others. If this is true for you, then perhaps you realize how important it is to try to understand as much as possible about the process in which you are so totally involved now and will be for the rest of your life.

ASPECTS OF THE COMMUNICATION PROCESS

A very important word in the paragraph above is *process*—the communication process. What does the word *process* mean to you? In the first place a process is dynamic —it is constantly moving. A process cannot be thought of as a "thing"—something static or unchanging. In order to think of a process as a thing or an entity, it is necessary to stop the process at some point and look at what is there at that particular moment. And what would be there at that moment is not the process itself but some part or component of the process. So, when we speak of the communication process we are speaking of a dynamic, ever-changing, ongoing event. From this perspective, then, does it seem more accurate to say we are studying the process of communicat*ing* rather than communicat*ion?* On the other hand, if we both know what we mean, does it matter what we call it?

Think about that for a minute. You and I are now involved in the process of communication. What is the purpose of this process? Through the use of words, we are attempting to *produce* meaning. If we fail to do this, our communication will not have been successful. You will not "understand" what I am trying to say even if you "understand" each word I am communicating to you. You and I will not hold the same meaning. Communication, then, can be thought of as a dynamic process the purpose of which is the creation of meaning.

Think of a movie you have seen recently. It would not really be correct to say that the movie "had" meaning. It would be better to say that the screenwriter was attempting to *evoke* meaning in you through his presentation of various characters, dialogues, and situations. If the movie "had" meaning, we would not all have so many disagreements about what the movie "meant." (Or how many times have you said to a friend "That's not what I meant" regardless of what the words you used seemed to mean to her.)

If the basic purpose of communication is thought of as being the creation of meaning, then, on a much larger scale, communication is a continuous, lifelong process for all of us. In communicating with our world and with others in it, we are constantly trying to create meaning; in other words, we are attempting to understand what is going on around us.

When viewed in this way, the process of communication appears much more complex than we originally might have supposed. There are many more parts or components to this process than we might have guessed. In attempting to understand and study this process and all its parts, researchers have devised many theoretical and visual methods, or models, for discussing and depicting the process of communication. A look at several of these might help draw together some aspects of the communication process which seem important if we are to understand how we do communicate.

MODELS OF COMMUNICATION

Think of the kinds of models with which you are familiar. There are models of cars and airplanes; there are models of the human skelton, or of different parts of the human body like the larynx or the ear; there is the eye, which often has been compared functionally to the operation of a camera; there is the globe; and there are also larger constructions which move in a way to depict the movement of the various planets in our solar system. We could go on and on giving examples of models, but those given above may be enough to suggest that all models are used to *represent* something—they are symbolic representations of structures, objects, or operations. In other words, a model may be used to show the size, shape, and relationship of various parts of an object or process, or to demonstrate how a system works. In the latter case it is not necessary that the model look like the system it represents but only that it function in as similar a way as possible.

From the examples given above one can see that models are useful in understanding an object or system under study.

Even though the earth does not "look like" the globe—China is not really bright orange, nor can one touch a line of longitude—still it helps us to understand the general shape of our planet, relationships between various continents, the relative size and location of oceans and seas. If we were to build a model which looked *exactly* like the earth, we would have gained nothing!

Like any other symbolic representation, a model helps us to see some things clearly, but in so doing prevents us from being aware of other things. Thus, in the development and study of models, one constantly must be alert to the possibility of misrepresentation (like an ancient map depicting a flat earth) and bias—know what aspects were included and what aspects were omitted. A distorted model can lead to misguided thinking and study of the object or process being investigated.

The following are models which show how several researchers have conceived of the communication process. While you read about these models, consider what aspects of the communication process each writer has chosen to include, what he has chosen to omit, and in each case whether or not you think those aspects included and those omitted are important.

The Shannon and Weaver Model

One of the earliest models of the communication process was that of Claude Shannon and Warren Weaver. Although the model was not intended originally to represent face-to-face human communication, it has been used by many in that way. Looking at the model, we can see an **information source,** a **transmitter,** the two arrows **signal** and **received signal** representing the channel, a **receiver,** and a **destination,** with one message being transmitted and one being received. In strictly vocal human communication, one might think of the information source and transmitter as being the brain and vocal apparatus respectively. The channel would be the surrounding air. The signal would be the sound waves received by the hearing mechanism of the person to whom one is speaking, and which are subsequently relayed to the brain, the destination.

In using this model for face-to-face human communication, many writers have combined the information source and the transmitter into simply the *encoder.* This term stands for the person who encodes—puts into language—a message. The encoder then sends this message across a channel, the air, to another person, the *decoder,* who receives the message and interprets or decodes to get the meaning. The important terms to remember are *encoder, message, channel,* and *decoder,* for they represent major variables in all other kinds of human communication. For example, if one uses a certain gesture and another sees this gesture, the first person has sent a message across a visual channel for the other to decode.

The one important element of the Shannon and Weaver model which we have not yet discussed is the **noise source** which feeds into the channel. In one sense the aspect of noise is very easy to understand because it means simply that there is outside interference or noise during the trans-

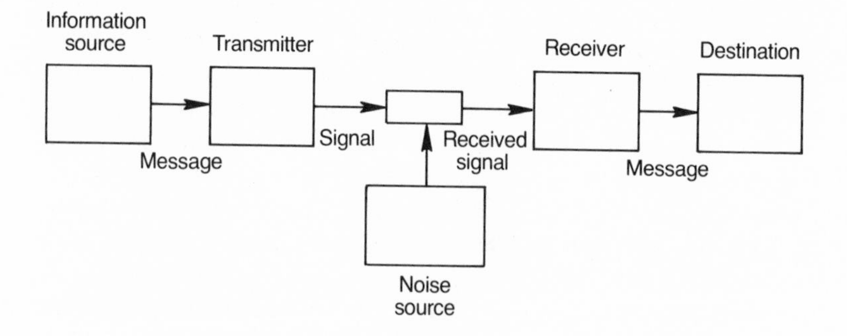

Figure 1. *The Shannon and Weaver Model of Communication*

mission of a message. Examples of this type of noise would be static on the radio or telephone. We all have experienced this kind of noise and know that, until it reaches a certain level, it does not necessarily interfere with our sending or receiving messages. When this point is reached, however, we may retune the radio or hang up the receiver because we can no longer hear correctly.

There are more subtle kinds of interference, however, which may be thought of as noise since they do affect the fidelity of message transmission and reception. How often have you sat in a classroom and, because of the way the teacher talked or moved, were unable to concentrate on what was being said? Or you may have had trouble paying attention because you were thinking about what you were going to do after class, that night, or the following weekend. These examples indicate that there are many sources of "noise" which can affect how well a message travels from sender, or encoder, to receiver, or decoder. The next time you are having trouble paying attention to someone who is trying to communicate with you, try to decide if it is because there is some kind of "noise" interfering.

The Dance Model

While the Shannon and Weaver model was very important in stimulating thought and research on the nature of communication, researchers soon realized that the linear nature of the communication process suggested by the model was not really representative of a great deal of human communication. Work in cybernetics, which began at about the same time that the Shannon and Weaver model was introduced, provided what many thought to be a missing element in the model.

Rather than being a linear process, human communication might be thought of as a circular process in which information about previous communications is fed back into the process. In other words, if I speak to you, very often your reply will be a response to what I said and my reply to you will be a response to what you said, ad infinitum. The important element here is the idea of *feedback*—one person's response to the other indicating positive or negative attitudes and feelings toward what the first person has said or toward the speaker in general. Based upon this feedback, the first person formulates her next response, which then serves as feedback to the second person. Obviously all feedback is not verbal. Think about the many different ways one person receives information from another, which lets her know how the other feels about her and what she is saying. One of the most blatant forms of feedback is simply walking away from a person while she is speaking, although the speaker and the listener may not assign the same meaning to the act. (For example, you are speaking to an acquaintance about your feelings on women's liberation. Suddenly he walks away. You assume he disagrees with the entire movement and considers you an idiot; actually, he had just spotted a friend he had not seen for five years about to board a bus.)

In human communication lineality is not *really* representative of what happens much of the time. According to Frank Dance, however, neither is circularity, because human communication does not go back to where it started from as a circle would indicate. Dance presented a model of communication which looks like a continuing spiral or helix. He explains his model as follows:

> At any and all times, the helix gives geometrical testimony to the concept that communication while moving forward is at the same moment coming back upon itself and being affected by its past behavior, for the coming curve of the helix is fundamentally affected by the curve from which it emerges.[1]

Thus, for Dance, communication is an ever-continuing, forward-moving process, each moment of which is determined largely by what has happened previously.

Figure 2. *The Dance Helical Model of Communication*

By looking at the Shannon and Weaver and the Dance models we can see those aspects of the communication process which each author has attempted to stress. In some ways the Dance model may be thought of as a modification of the Shannon and Weaver model, and although the Shannon and Weaver model includes specific components of the process, both models attempt to represent the way in which the communication process works.

The Berlo Model

Although most communication theorists consider communication to be a process, all do not develop models which represent that process, or give a picture of how communication works. The SMCR (**S**ource, **M**essage, **C**hannel, **R**eceiver) model developed by David Berlo presents the "ingredients of communication," or those aspects which are present in any communication event; but he does not attempt to represent the actual process. Berlo explains that any attempt to indicate which of these elements precedes another would destroy the basic process nature of communication because in a process all elements affect each other, and sequential interrelations within a true process are impossible to determine. As Berlo states, "A chicken is what an egg makes in order to reproduce itself."[2]

As you can see, Berlo's model is in some respects similar to that of Shannon and Weaver insofar as components of the process are concerned. According to Berlo, all communication events will have a source, a message, a channel which carries the message, and a receiver. Berlo is interested in discovering what factors help to determine the effectiveness (or ineffectiveness) of communication, in other words, what elements influence (or affect) the noise factor. Under each of his ingredients of communication, he has indicated several factors people should be aware of when studying the process of communication—particularly a specific communication act. If there seems to be a breakdown in communication, can the cause of this be found by examining the various factors under each element? For ex-

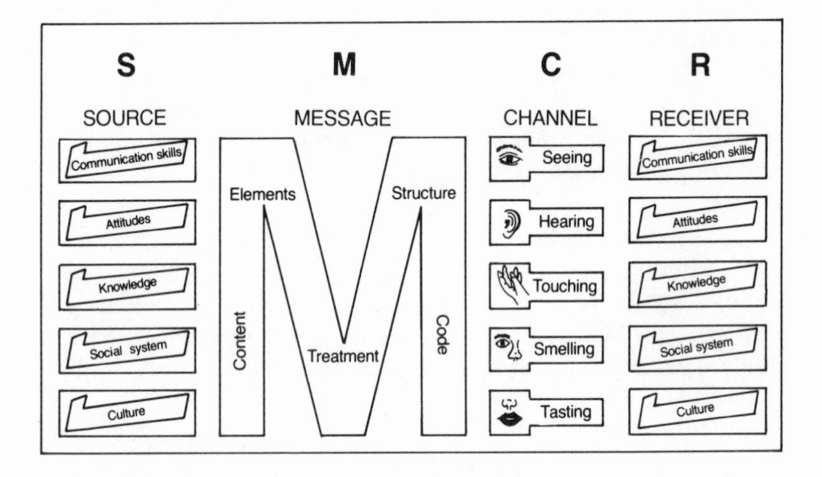

Figure 3. *The Berlo SMCR Model of Communication*

ample, if you and a friend do not seem to be getting anywhere in trying to resolve a problem, is it because one of you is not very skilled at communication? Or does one of you have an attitude toward self or others which prevents effective communication? Or should you just abandon all talk, throw your arms around each other, and go for a walk?

Summary

Each of the models discussed so far has its strengths and weaknesses which both help and hinder us in attempting to understand the process of communication. Which of the three models seems to you to be most helpful? What specific things about the communication process does each model include? omit? If you were to develop your own model, what would it look like? Take several minutes and design a model. Now examine what you have done. Are you satisfied with the things you have included and omitted?

The last model we will study is very different from the first three. It asks us to consider certain aspects of the communication process which really have not been included in the others. Although in some ways it is a more complicated model, it may be more helpful to you in your attempt to understand more about how *you* communicate.

THE BARNLUND MODEL

The Theoretical Foundations

Earlier in this chapter we said that things do not *have* meaning—*people* have meaning for them. As we communicate, we attempt to develop meaning within ourselves and others so that we each "mean" the same thing. In fact, we spend a great deal of our time trying to understand things, in other words give them meaning. When that friendly-looking young man or woman sitting across from you in the library smiles at you, does that mean he or she would like to get to know you? thinks you also have just seen a funny thing happen across the aisle? is recalling a funny experience which happened the night before? And why did you decide in the first place that he or she was friendly? Did someone sitting next to you say "She (or he) is a good friend of mine and is really a friendly person"? Probably not. You most likely picked up facial or body cues from this person which to you usually *mean* "friendly."

According to Dean Barnlund, "The word *communication* stands for those acts in which meaning develops within human beings . . . ,"[3] and as the first of seven communication postulates which constitute the theoretical foundation of his model he says, "Communication Describes the Evolution of Meaning."[4] When we speak with another person, when we watch events going on around us, often when we sit and think about ourselves, what we are doing is attempting to *reduce our uncertainty*, to understand, to give meaning. As Barnlund says, "It is not a reaction to something, nor an interaction with something, but a *transaction* [emphasis added] in which man invents and attributes meanings to realize his purposes."[5] He calls his model the Transactional Model of Communication.

The idea that meaning *evolves* during communication is not an easy idea to accept. We tend to think that actions, words, symbols, events, have a definite meaning which we either attempt to discover or, if we "know" what they mean, try to convince others to agree with. During the presidential inauguration of 1973 I was in Washington, D.C. There were at least two very distinct groups in the city that day. One group was celebrating the second inauguration of Richard Nixon. Another was protesting it. Neither group could understand the actions of the other because each group had a different meaning for it and other events that occured that day.

We also have discussed Barnlund's second communication postulate. It is that "Communication Is Dynamic."[6] Communication is a *dynamic process* during which meaning is evolved, and this evolution is based upon a selective method of "seeing." When we meet a new person, we *select* certain cues about that person to focus on. Once we have made this selection, we refer these cues to our storehouse of past experiences and develop a meaning for this new person. Of course, this all happens very quickly and we are usually quite unaware of the process. In many ways this is good; otherwise, we would be very much like the millipede who, when asked to describe how he walked, stood still, unable to move any one of his thousand legs! On the other hand, as we said before in discussing the values and limitations of models of communication, when certain aspects of an event or process (or person) are selected and focused on, others are inevitably ignored even though they may be more important. This, probably, is one reason why first impressions are so often if not completely wrong, rarely completely right. Not only may we have selected unimportant cues, we may have assigned a completely different meaning to the cue than the person herself assigns to it.

This entire process is fun to play around with. The next time you meet a new person (perhaps one of the people sitting next to you in class), try to discover exactly what cues you picked out as being important about that person. Eyes? Hair? Dress? Voice? Why did you select the things you did? What meaning did you give to what you chose? Why? Might another person assign entirely diffrent meanings? What would your best friend say? Your mother or father? The instructor?

The evolution of meaning is a continuous dynamic process in which each of us is always involved. This is Barnlund's third postulate—"Communication Is Continuous."[7] As he says, it is a "condition of life" just like breathing, and as our breathing fluctuates depending upon our activity, so does our communication with our world; we evolve meaning with our world, others, and ourselves according to our needs of the moment.

The fourth communication postulate underlying the theoretical foundation of Barnlund's Transactional Model of Communication is "Communication Is Circular."[8] This should not be confused, however, with our earlier discussion of the impossibility of communication going back to where it started and repeating itself. What Barnlund is arguing against is the traditional linear model of communication as represented in the Shannon and Weaver model. If, as Barnlund says, communication is viewed ". . . as a continuous process of evolving meanings,"[9] then it makes no sense to view communication as having a starting point in a speaker, or encoder, and an ending point in a listener, or decoder. Using these same terms, one person may be simultaneously encoder and decoder in that he is constantly developing meaning either with the other person or event in the communication situation or entirely within himself. In other words, if meaning evolves during the process of communication, then we cannot say that one "sends" meaning to another who "receives" it. Rather together the people involved generate the meaning in any particular communication situation.

That Barnlund does not view communication as being circular as Dance discussed circularity becomes even more apparent in his fifth postulate: "Communication Is Unrepeatable."[10] If you see a friend and say "Hi! What's up?" and immediately say again "Hi! What's up?" these two communications, exactly the same and separated only by seconds, obviously will have very different meanings to your friend. In the first case he would probably have assumed you "meant" that you see him and are recognizing this fact. Your friend was probably ready to do the same by saying "Nothing!" In the second case the "meaning" will be very different. To your friend it may "mean" that you have been studying too hard and obviously need a rest (or that you are doing one of those communication experiments again!). Communication is unrepeatable, really, because we are unrepeatable. The you that went to sleep last night is not the same you that woke up this morning.

As human beings we are changeable. Because of outside events and inside experiences we are not the same from moment to moment. Thus, a friend can say something to you today and you will laugh. She can say the same thing two weeks from now and you might be hurt and question the relationship. In other words identical input does not always produce identical output. In most communication situations, no matter how similar, different meanings are created.

Because of new meanings in each new situation, "Communication Is Irreversible"[11]—Barnlund's sixth postulate. One cannot go backwards and "unmean" a meaning which evolved. From the time we are born until we die we constantly move forward and cannot go back to some original point. To use Barnlund's example, some processes are repeatable and reversible. Ice when heated becomes water then steam. Reverse the process and you have ice again. But communication is not this kind of process. If you said something very unkind to a friend yesterday and today regret your comment, you cannot return to that moment yesterday before you opened your mouth. All you can do is keep going forward by apologizing or saying "Forget I ever said that" (which, of course, he can never *really* do); your friend, too, is constantly moving (or living) forward and can only forgive and go on from there.

Barnulund's seventh and last communication postulate is "Communication Is Complex."[12] By this he means that when one considers all the different situations in which meaning is evolved, the many different ways in which verbal and nonverbal communication can occur—within one person, between a person and the environment, between two or among many people, among organizations and societies, and the infinite number of reasons we have for communicating in an equally great number of different situations, we see that communication is very complex indeed. When we say that we are going to study communication, we have set for ourselves quite a task!

The Transactional Model of Communication

To simplify the study of communication, Barnlund has constructed the Transactional Model of Communication. The model represents symbolically the nature of a communication situation which, as we have said before, is a situation in which there is an evolution or development of meaning.

Figure 4 depicts a simple communication situation. The darkened circle labeled **P**₁ (Person 1) can represent you sitting alone in an outer office waiting for a job interview.* Looking around, you see many different items or cues. You decode (**D**), or assign meaning to some of these cues, and encode (**E**) this meaning by your verbal and nonverbal reactions. (In this case, no one is there to see these reactions as is the case when a communication situation involves more than one person.) As Barnlund says, "The spiral line connecting encoding and decoding processes is used to

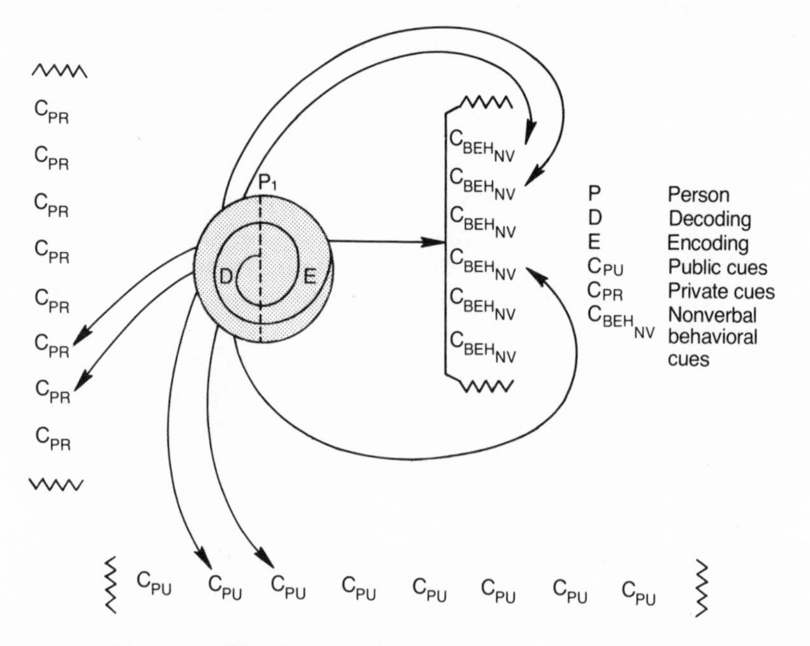

Figure 4. *The Transactional Model of Communication (One Person)*

* In his original explanation of the model, Barnlund used the example of a patient entering a doctor's office.

give diagrammatic representation to the continuous, unrepeatable, and irreversible nature of communication that was postulated earlier."[13]

While you are sitting in the office, there are several different kinds of cues which you may select and assign meaning to. There are cues which are *public* and are represented by the letters $\mathbf{C}_{PU}$ across the bottom of the model. Think about what kinds of things in the office you would label as public. The furniture? The pictures on the wall? The rain falling outside the window? If you guessed these kinds of things, you are absolutely right. Public cues are those which would be available to anyone entering the office, which were there before you and others got there, and over which you and others just entering have no control. In the model the arrows coming out from you to the public cues indicate that you will be *assigning* meaning to them; they will not *present* meaning to you. For example, on the wall you see a large poster showing a hand with the index and middle finger raised. To you this *means* "peace" and you decide that the people in this office may be O.K. You have just assigned meaning not only to the poster but also to the people who work in the office. If a person twenty or so years older than you were to enter the office and see the poster, he might decide this *means* "victory" as it did during World War II and decide the people in the office were somewhat out of date. Public cues, then, are those things which are available for anyone entering the situation to see. Some of these we pick out and assign meaning to; others we may be unaware of.

Imagine now that while still sitting in the office you feel the palms of your hands sweating and your throat tightening. To you this *means* that you are becoming nervous about the job interview. If others were to enter the office, they would not know about your sweaty palms and uncomfortable throat. These are known as private cues and are represented in the model by the letters $\mathbf{C}_{PR}$ along the left side of the page. You will notice that as with the public cues, the arrows in the model are going from you to the private cues. Again, you are assigning meaning to these cues. Given the same cues in the same situation, another person might decide that the room is too warm and that she is smoking too much and must cut down. Public and private cues differ from one another in their availability to the people involved in a communication situation. They are similar, however, in that neither type is under the direct control of the people involved in the situation. You did not put the poster up and you did not order your hands to start sweating (nor can you order them to stop!).

The third set of cues depicted in the model are those over which you may have some degree of control. They are your nonverbal behaviors and are represented in figure 4 as $\mathbf{C}_{BEH_{NV}}$. You emit these cues as indicated by the arrow going from you, the encoder (**E**), to the $\mathbf{C}_{BEH}$ cues, and you also assign meaning to them as the other set of arrows going from you, the decoder (**D**), indicates. Since you are alone in the office, it is probable that you will not sit in your chair and talk! After waiting for forty-five minutes, however, you may give a long sigh followed by "Good grief!" In this case you have encoded a verbal behavioral cue (represented in figure 5 as $\mathbf{C}_{BEH_V}$), and the meaning you assign to this is that you are tired of waiting (or perhaps "Who do they think they are, anyway?"). Instead of doing this, you might look at your watch angrily which, although nonverbal, would probably be assigned the same meaning by you.

In this situation, there are probably many nonverbal behavioral cues of which you could become aware—for instance, how you dressed for the interview, how you combed your hair, how you are sitting in the office. And what meanings would you (and perhaps your interviewer) assign to all these cues? The jagged lines at each end of the list of $\mathbf{C}_{BEH}$ indicate that the number of verbal and nonverbal cues in this situation is open. The same is true for public and private cues.

Now imagine that a woman opens the inner office door

and enters the room where you are sitting. Adding another person does not change the appearance of the model very much (see figure 5).

As you can see, there are still the same types of cues which we discussed before available to each person. The only difference is that in this situation, each of you will be aware of the other person's presence and will begin deliberately to choose and control certain verbal and nonverbal behavioral cues which you emit. Each of you also will attempt to determine how the other person is evaluating the cues you

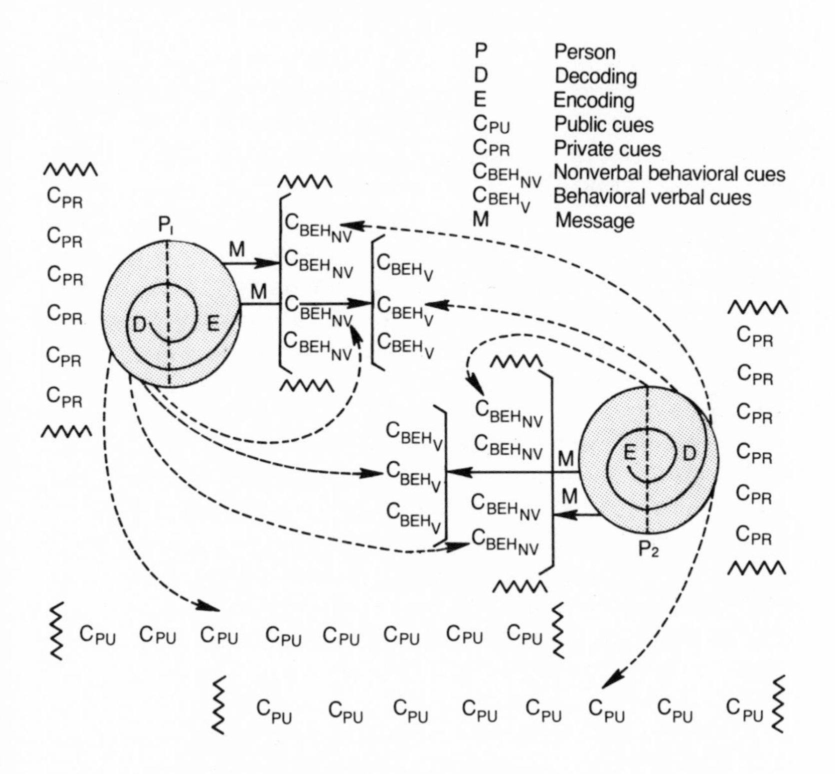

Figure 5. *The Transactional Model of Communication (Two People)*

do give. *When you begin to control the cues you emit and attempt to determine how the other person is evaluating these cues, your behavioral cues, both verbal and nonverbal, may be thought of as constituting a message.* This is represented in the model by **M**, and the arrow related to this **M** going from $\mathbf{P}_1$ and $\mathbf{P}_2$ to their verbal and nonverbal behavioral cues indicates that you and the other person in the situation are encoding behavioral cues or interpersonal messages. As you also can see from the arrows going from $\mathbf{P}_1$ and $\mathbf{P}_2$, each person is decoding, or assigning meaning to, both his or her own messages and those of the other person.

Some examples might help to make all this a little clearer. As stated, you have been waiting in the outer office for a long time. Suddenly, a woman appears from the inner office. You look at her, and after glancing around the office, she looks at you. All of the public cues—the poster, the furniture, and so on—which have been available to you also are available to her, although at this point you have no way of knowing if she sees any of these things and, if she does, what meaning she assigns to them. She does not have access to any of your private cues. She asks, "Are you ____?" And you reply "Yes" and stand up. So far there have been only five words exchanged between you, but think of all the interpersonal messages, or behavioral cues, which are available! Certainly you and probably she give some meaning to her personal appearance and to the way in which she walked from the inner office and toward you ($\mathbf{C}_{BEH_{NV}}$). Beyond the "simple meaning" of her question ($\mathbf{C}_{BEH_V}$), you may both have given meaning to *the way* in which she asked the question ($\mathbf{C}_{BEH_{NV}}$). The kinds of meanings you have already given to her cues will determine to some extent the kinds of meanings you give to your own behavioral cues. If she seems to be a warm and friendly person, you may react to her with less nervousness than you had expected and see the way in which you stood up ($\mathbf{C}_{BEH_{NV}}$) and responded to her ($\mathbf{C}_{BEH_V}$) as meaning that you are confident of yourself. You also will be attempting to decide how she evaluated your behavior by watching her verbal and nonverbal behavioral cues *while* you are responding to her and then as she responds to you in turn. There is, of course, no way of knowing exactly how another person is evaluating us, but, with varying degrees of success, we all try.

You can take this little episode on for yourself. Even though this has been a relatively simple communication situation, think of all the cues and messages that have been available. Imagine how many more there will be as the two of you shake hands, walk into her office, exchange small talk, and then begin the interview. If there are so many cues available in a situation as simple as this one, no wonder we sometimes feel sightly confused when going into a room where a party is already in progress or meeting a group of total strangers! As we said before, communication definitely is complex.

CONCLUSION

So far, we have talked about the communication process in general, and have presented several models of communication in the hope that these will help you develop a general idea of what is included in the process. Finally, we have presented in detail Barnlund's Transactional Model of Communication and have illustrated how this model can be used in studying everyday situations.

In the following chapters we will discuss various aspects of the communication process. Some of the chapters you may find more interesting than others, but in each case try to keep yourself in your reading. In other words, we are going to be talking about how communication works. See if along the way you can learn not only more about the process in general, but specifically about how *you* communicate. You will be spending a great deal of your time for the rest of your life communicating with others, so learning more about *your own* communication is certainly as important as and probably more important than simply learning some terms and theories about the process. And since you are the most important topic of this book, the next chapter will deal with your body and how you use it in exchanging information with your world.

NOTES

1. Frank E. X. Dance, "Toward a Theory of Human Communication," in *Human Communication Theory,* ed. Frank E. X. Dance (New York: Holt, Rinehart, and Winston, 1967), p. 296.
2. David K. Berlo, *The Process of Communication* (New York: Holt, Rinehart, and Winston, 1960), p. 38.
3. Dean C. Barnlund, "A Transactional Model of Communication," in *Language Behavior: A Book of Readings in Communication,* comp. Johnnye Aken, Alvin Goldberg, Gail Myers, and John Stewart. (The Hague: Mouton, 1970), p. 47.
4. Ibid.
5. Ibid.
6. Ibid., p. 48.
7. Ibid.
8. Ibid., p. 49.
9. Ibid.
10. Ibid., p. 51.
11. Ibid.
12. Ibid., p. 52.
13. Ibid., p. 53.

2 CHANNELS OF COMMUNICATION

> Trying to stop all thinking is like looking into one mirror reflecting another mirror. To get free of the whirl I have to step into my senses.
>
> Hugh Prather, *I Touch the Earth, The Earth Touches Me.**

What does it mean to step into one's senses? Suppose you are upset and a friend touches your shoulder to let you know she is with you and will help if she can. At another time a certain smell in the air seems to tell you the ocean is nearby even if you cannot yet see it. Or perhaps before spreading a hot sauce over your food, you first taste a bit to see if you like it. Sense organs in our bodies act as receivers of stimulation, and as we become aware of this stimulation, we develop a meaning for it and act accordingly; in other words, we *respond.* Obviously, we do not respond to every stimulus in our environment. If we did, we could be immobilized because of the excess of information! Rather, we select certain stimuli to attend to and ignore many others.

Recall the interview described in the first chapter. We said you might notice the furniture, the poster on the wall, the rain falling outside, your sweaty hands and tight throat, and your interviewer's personal appearance. Think of all the things you may not have noticed: the feel of the thick carpet as you walked to the chair; the smell of false air indicating that the air conditioner was on; the feel of the vinyl chair you were sitting in—at first cold and gradually warmer and warmer until your clothing began to stick to you; the taste of your salty lips as you tried to keep them moist; the muted sound of a typewriter coming from some inner office.

Where are you right now? Look around you; feel around you; taste, smell, and hear around you. What are you aware of now that you were not before? Can you step into your senses and become aware of things going on around and inside of you which you may not have noticed previously?

Right now I am sitting on the grass in the middle of Central Park in New York City. All around me I can see the grass and the trees and the ring of high buildings surrounding the park. Off to my right I can see a woman with a baby carriage and a boy in a blue shirt playing with a collie. I can also see two ants slowly crossing my leg and wonder why I could not feel them until I first saw them.

From all directions I can hear the sound of people playing various games—there are shouts, whistles, laughs, grunts, cries—and the familiar sound of a siren on one of the streets around the park. I can feel the grass tickling my legs and the wind blowing my hair and brushing past my face and arms—sometimes more and sometimes less. I can also feel my left leg going to sleep which tells me I should change positions. I can smell the grass which must have been mown recently and the smoke from the cigarette of a man sitting nearby. I can also smell the heat of the day, and I am not sure what that means. I can taste the smoke from my own cigarette and now the cold tingle of my canned orange soda. I can also taste my mouth which somehow seems very familiar. And as I try to concentrate on all these things, I realize how much I usually miss, and I wonder what things I am still unaware of.

And now I hear the sound of a radio telling me it is 12:15, which means I should go home and fix some lunch, and I marvel at the fact that somehow this information was more important than the increasingly empty feeling in my stomach. I feel the day getting warmer and warmer, and I both long for my air-conditioned apartment and dislike the thought of giving up my pleasant grassy spot.

THE SENSES

So far we have been talking about the five most common senses: sight, sound, touch, smell and taste. It is now understood that there are more than these five senses. For example, we also have a kinesthetic or muscle sense and a vestibular or balance sense and perhaps more. Since our primary goal, however, is not to understand the physiological operations of the body but rather to become aware of the many ways we communicate with others and with our world, we will limit our discussion to the five senses with which most of us are already familiar. Becoming more aware of each of these five senses may be no small task. Due in large part to our culture, we get most of our information from our eyes and ears. Recently a friend of mine could not tell me if the food in a newly opened restaurant was any good even though he had eaten there several days before. It seems he was having an interesting conversation during lunch and had completely forgotten to taste any of his food! This entire section is dedicated to him and to the rest of us who have no idea how a hot summer day sounds, tastes, and smells.

Sight

All of us have some knowledge about the structure and operation of the eye. Although it is often compared with a camera, we know that it does not really function like a camera. The eye does not produce pictures in the brain but rather it supplies the brain, finally, with chains of electrical impulses which in the brain represent objects. The process of producing such "pictures" is based upon a number of factors—for example, our past experience with similar objects, our emotional state at a given moment, the physical aspects, for example, illumination, at any particular time, and changes in the object being viewed.

With close to 70 percent of all the body's sense receptors located in the eyes, it is difficult not to regard the eye as our most important sense organ. Think for a moment of the amount of information you receive through your eyes. Glance up from this page and look around you. Compare the amount of information you received from all your other sense organs combined.

The eyes often have been called the distance, or long-range, sense organs. We usually can see things much farther away than we can hear them and certainly much farther than we can feel, taste, or smell them. They are, then, our most important sense for protection and defense. You might try to imagine your predicament if you had to wait to smell some suspicious-looking person approaching you on the street!

Seeing also supplies us with most of our information about the size and shape of an object. You may be familiar with the tale of the six blind men who attempted to describe what an elephant looks like. To each man the elephant "looked like" whatever part of its anatomy he happened to touch. Imagine trying to describe what a snow drift looks like if all you were allowed was a touch of the snow. Or the Grand Canyon from a touch of the stone—or even several thousand touches!

In addition to that of size and shape, vision seems to add to our perception of detail even when an entire object may be touched. I have on my desk what used to be a clear solid glass block which a friend gave me several years ago. The block now has developed hundreds of cracks so that it looks very much like frost on a window pane. When I rub the glass without looking at it, it feels relatively smooth. When I look at the glass and rub it, however, I can feel the hundreds of tiny cracks. This perception of detail, of course, also works the other way around. The cotton ball you see on the dresser only *looks* soft because you have felt other cotton balls and soft things so that you know what soft things "look like."

We could go on and on about the kinds of information you receive from your eyes. For example, even though a few people over the years have claimed to be able to feel or hear colors, no one seems to have been able to prove that any of us perceives color except by seeing color. That your green and my green may not be the same thing is an interesting idea to pursue, but for now let us just say that without your vision sense, you would live in a black and white rather than a technicolor world—whatever those colors may be for you.

As we have seen, our eyes supply us with a great deal of information; however, like our other sense organs, they miss a great deal more than they take in. We live in a sea of electromagnetic waves ranging in size from mile-long radio waves to the tiny ultraviolent ones. Yet, it is possible for us with an unaided eye to see only a very, very small portion of the radiation around us. In addition to physical limitations, we tend to select certain things to see and to ignore others. This selection process occurs largely in the brain, and we will talk more about this in the next chapter on perception.

For now let us concentrate on what we do see, and determine if we can increase the amount of information we receive from our eyes. Select one object close to you. Take several minutes and just look at that object. If you want, move either it or yourself so you can see it from all angles. Let your eyes roam all over the object—do not just stare. Now, what do you see? Are there color or texture variations which you had not noticed before? Does the object look very different from one angle than from another? If you did not know what the object was, how heavy would you guess it to be? Without being too annoying, you might try this exercise using a very good friend and see what you have not seen previously about her or him.

Hearing

The second sense organ through which we receive a great deal of information is the ear. In fact, many people are now living in areas of the country where much time and effort are being expended to try to reduce the amount of sound people are exposed to during any given day.

Again, we are not concerned about how, physiologically, the ear functions. Most of us know that, in general, sound waves are gathered in by the outer ear and funneled into the eardrum which, when vibrating, sets the three small bones of the middle ear into motion which then pass the energy along through the fluid in the inner ear, where the impulses are picked up by small hair cells and are passed along to the brain. We also know that the sound waves picked up by the outer ear are generated by some sort of motion, usually that of a vibrating object, and that sound waves are really movements of the air particles surrounding the object. As these waves travel out from the object, very much like the ripples radiating out from a stone thrown into water, they can vary in several ways, primarily in their height, giving us differences in amplitude or loudness, and in the distances between the waves, giving us the frequency or pitch.

Now, this all sounds very elementary and in one respect it is. But think about the process just described. What sounds do you hear right now? Try to imagine these different sounds as actually being differences in the movements of the air particles. It is not an easy thing to understand. You might also try to imagine yourself in outer space, where there is no sound because there is no air.

Hearing, like sight, is a distance receptor. Unlike sight, however, it is not only a space sense but also a localizing sense. If you have a child, or a younger brother or sister, or even a pet you probably have learned that a certain tiny sound means the person or the animal is in a specific place doing a specific thing. Your ability to identify and localize the sound may be greatest when someone or something is in need of help or when some misdemeanor is being committed. I have a great gray Persian cat named Pooh. From two rooms away I can now hear that Pooh is in the process of very gently unrolling an entire roll of toilet paper and I am sure no one else would hear this sound and know exactly what it was.

Sounds come from various and specific parts of our total visual environment. Our acoustic environment usually is not completely filled, as is our visual environment, even though at times it may seem to be. One of the joys of many of our newer stereo systems may be that they give us a uniformly filled acoustic space.

As we all know, however, people deal with their own acoustic space very differently; many people may not like 360° stereo systems *because* they fill the space. Some people go to great lengths to cut down on the amount of sound by reducing the surfaces from which sound can reverberate. We have acoustic tiling for walls and ceilings and we put rugs and draperies in our homes and apartments to cut down on the amount of reverberated sound. The sound of walking across the floor in a totally empty room arouses such a strong feeling for many of us that movie producers can use this one technique to convey all kinds of moods.

We also differ in the kinds of sounds we pay attention to and ignore. If you are at home now, notice the kinds of sounds with which you have surrounded yourself. Do you have a radio on? Records? Nothing? For some people sounds from either a radio or from records would be so distracting that they could not concentrate on anything else, while for others these sounds are necessary. At the moment I have an air conditioner on, not only to make it cooler but also to block out the noises from outside and from the adjacent apartment. I cannot, however, sleep with the air conditioner on because the sound bothers me. Obviously, then, it is possible to use one sound to mask or block out another sound, and it is also possible to completely ignore some sounds. That people's abilities and preferences differ in each of these respects helps to explain why your "sounds" may be another person's "noise."

As we said before, the noise factor has become an important topic in many areas of the country and hopefully will be given more attention. For some time we have known that too much noise can affect a person's hearing. A recent study in New York, however, has suggested that too much noise may also affect a child's learning ability. We may already have come to a point where, because of the amount of noise we are becoming used to, a certain amount is necessary. You may have heard about the quiet typewriter which was a complete failure. It seems that the secretaries using it needed the constant clacking in order to feel they were accomplishing anything! This may not be so different from the feeling many of us have that in order to be good, a party must be *loud.*

Think for a moment about your own acoustic space. Think about how much time you spend listening to others talk—friends, parents, teachers, newscasters, sports announcers. Think about the music you listen to and perhaps play. Think about some of your very favorite sounds, like the surf breaking gently as it rolls onto a beach, and some of your least favorite sounds like an air hammer pounding a concrete sidewalk. Think about all the daily sounds which you do notice and all the ones of which you are unaware. Listen for a minute and try to hear *everything* there is to hear. As we get older our acuteness for particularly high frequency sounds falls off sharply. Although we cannot halt this process, we can train ourselves to become more aware of all the sounds we are physically able to hear.

Touch

When we speak of touch as one of the five senses, what do we mean? It might be more appropriate to say that we are going to talk about the haptic system, which takes into account the sense organs in the skin which react to touch and pressure, temperature, and pain, as well as those in the muscles, joints, and tendons which give feelings of motion, position, and tension. For example, right now try to become aware of how your clothes feel as they are touching your skin. Can you feel that some materials are soft and some rough? With your finger, gently rub the tip of your nose. How does this feel on both your finger and your nose? Then, concentrate on how your body feels in whatever position you are in at the moment. Are your arms or legs bent? From inside, try to feel your shoulders and arms. Is there any tension in either or both of these places?

Technically we could talk about two different "feeling" systems. Since we are more interested in how we experience the information provided by our various sense organs, however, and since the external and internal systems often are experienced very similarly, we will group everything together in talking about touch, and usually we will mean those times when we come into some kind of contact with our external environment.

As mentioned before, the skin has three kinds of sensitivity: touch and pressure, temperature, and pain. It is not, however, uniformly sensitive to each kind of stimulation. Different regions of the body have different numbers of receptors sensitive to each of the three kinds of stimuli. All of us know some parts of our body which are more sensitive to being touched than others. This simply means that there are more "touch receptors" in such places. See if you can discover which regions of your body are more sensitive to temperature. If you have a match, light it, blow it out, then quickly touch the palm of your hand, the back of your hand, the tip of your index finger. Do the same thing again, but this time touch the bottom of your foot, then the top, and then your kneecap. Learning exactly where on your body you are most sensitive to different kinds of stimulation can add pleasure and avoid displeasure in many ways.

All living creatures react to being touched, poked, or

pressed. As with each other sense, however, various lower animals have a much more highly developed sense of touch than do humans. While we can say that our sense of touch enables us to feel our way around in the world, this statement is very literally true for many organisms whose antennae, protrusions, or small hairs are their primary sources for receiving information from their environment.

This is not to say, obviously, that the various sense receptors in the skin are not important to humans. Probably all of us have had the experience of feeling something hurting without having first seen the cause of the pain. For example, we know when new sandals are beginning to rub a blister without seeing the leather rubbing or the welt forming. This ability to feel pain is one of our primary defenses against injury, and for those few people who lack such ability, everyday living is a dangerous proposition. Similarly, in a protective sense our temperature receptors are important, as you may have discovered earlier with the match. In fact, the perception of temperature is so important to us that we seem to be able to perceive changes of less than one hundredth of a degree.

We also use the sense receptors in our skin in hundreds of less dramatic ways. Think of the number of times today you used touch for identification or recognition such as for finding a quarter in your pocket or hunting for a pen in your bag or for additional information such as brushing over your hair to find out how it "looks." The last example suggests that many things we touch, we do not *just* touch but rather rub in some way. Whereas we can feel the temperature of an object simply by touching it, we cannot feel its texture this way. With your finger, touch something around you. Is it smooth, rough, fine grained, coarse? Now rub your finger back and forth over the object. It is probably now much easier for you to describe its texture accurately.

This same principle applies to our awareness of things touching us. It is probably a blessing that we are not constantly aware of the feel of our clothing against our skin. It is beneficial, however, that we can feel the tickle of a bee moving slowly up our arm. In order for us to remain aware of a touch stimulus, it must be strong enough to attract our attention and it then must have a certain small rate of change. Remember the two ants that were crawling across my leg while I was sitting in the park? In that instance the stimulus was not strong enough to attract my attention. When I became visually aware of the ants, the rate of change in their crawling on my skin was great enough that I could then feel their movement.

We have seen how the sense receptors in the skin provide us with much useful information about our environment. The importance of certain kinds of stimulation seems to be evident quite early in the development of animals. You may be familiar with the experiments of Harry Harlow in which he placed baby monkeys in cages with both wire and cloth "mothers." Even when the wire mother provided the milk the baby needed, the small monkey chose to lie close to the cloth mother and would go to her in times of stress. In several cases, simply having contact with the soft terry cloth mother seemed to give the baby courage to explore strange objects placed in the cage.

Certain kinds of tactile stimulation for the human infant may be important in other ways. It has been suggested that lack of such stimulation may cause the child to have problems later in developing speech and proper symbolic recognition, and still later in learning more mature forms of tactile communication such as adequate sexual functioning.[1] Ashley Montagu even says that one of the reasons we may enjoy the kind of rock dancing which most of us either do or have done is that we did not receive adequate tactile stimulation when we were young![2]

Whether or not you want to go along with him on this point is really not the issue. The important thing is that the kind and amount of tactile stimulation each of us had as a child may have been important for the development of many of our later behavior patterns. Certainly as a child our awareness of self was based largely on tactile experiences. For this and other reasons, it is interesting to note that at least in our culture, it seems a mother is "permitted" to hold and fondle a girl baby far longer than a boy baby, and to speculate on the possible effects later in life of such different tactile experiences for woman and for men.

This is a cultural phenomenon, and there are differences between families within our culture as to the amount of touching which occurs. But does it not seem strange that, given how important tactile stimulation is, our culture tends to discourage physical contact between people unless they are involved in an intimate relationship? As one insightful woman has said:

> Society today tends to downgrade the sense of touch, equating it with manual as opposed to mental skills. In so doing society ignores the extent to which the combination of touch and intellect constitutes the art of the pianist or surgeon, sculptor or mechanic, inventor or magician—not to mention the few individuals, the safecracker, pickpocket, or card shark, who have misdirected their talents.[3]

You can probably add to this list examples of your own.

It is interesting to note, too, that of all the senses, touch involves us most intimately with whomever we are touching or whoever is touching us. Unlike seeing or hearing, we feel touch *inside* us, too. Even in taste and smell, the sensations remain on the surfaces of the mouth or nose. As Montagu has said,

> Although touch is not itself an emotion, its sensory elements induce those neural, glandular, muscular, and mental changes which in combination we call an emotion. Hence touch is not experienced as a simple physical modality, as sensation, but affectively, as emotion.[4]

If you doubt this, think about your *feelings* when someone you love gently touches you. You might also try to remember your feelings when, as a child, your mother or father spanked you.

That a touch seems to communicate more than, say, a glance can be illustrated by looking at some of the situations in which we avoid touch and in which we regulate touching behavior. For example, have you ever had anyone apologize to you for glancing at you? Yet how often have you exchanged apologies with someone because you inadvertently touched one another? And why is it that we will go to incredible lengths to avoid touching others on a crowded subway or bus even though we can see them, hear them, and smell them?

So far as regulating touch is concerned, think about the first few touches in the beginning of a new relationship that has the potential for becoming a romantic one. We may have sat and looked at and spoken to each other for several hours. Yet the first few touches may be made to appear very accidental indeed.

Think for a while about your own touching behavior and your awareness of touch. Many of us take the kinds of feelings we have been talking about very much for granted. It may be that one of the times we become most aware of our tactile feelings is when they are absent, as when a part of the body has been deadened with novocaine or when our foot falls asleep.

Again, try to become aware of how your body feels to you right now. Turn your head from side to side. Does your hair brush across any part of your neck or shoulders? If so, how does it feel? The hair on certain parts of our bodies greatly enhances our tactile sensitivity in those areas. With your finger, very gently rub the under side of your arm and then do the same on the top. Try this same thing again, but this time blow very gently on both places. Are the feelings different on the two sides?

Concentrate on how your clothes feel against your body. Although we can become aware of the sensation of their touching us, clothing for the most part cuts off lots of pleasurable experiences of our bodies being "touched" by other things, as anyone who has gone swimming both nude and clothed knows.

Think also of the different things you may do to your body which changes the way it feels when others touch it. Shaving, applying various creams, spraying hair sprays, ad infinitum, changes how we feel to others and how we feel inside when others touch us or when we touch ourselves.

Often when we talk about touch, we assume that we mean touching something with our fingers or hands, but there are many different ways of touching other than with the hands. Think about how you touch other people. Does it bother you to have your arms or legs touching those of someone you are sitting next to? Do you like to be held close and cuddled, or does this make you uncomfortable? In greetings, do you shake hands with some? Hug others? Kiss a few? If so, imagine switching around these people and forms of greetings. Interesting possibilities! It has been suggested that one of the rules in our culture is that a superior can touch a subordinate, but not vice versa. In other words a boss can touch a worker and a teacher can touch a student—theoretically, at least. In light of this it is interesting to note that in general, men can touch women, but a woman touching a man can be a different thing all together.

Montague has written that "the skin, like a cloak, covers us all over, the oldest and the most sensitive of our organs, our first medium of communication, and our most efficient of protectors. Perhaps, next to the brain, the skin is the most important of all our organ systems."[5] As a cloak, our skin does not separate us from our world so much as it connects us with it. Becoming more aware of all the information we can receive through our skin can be an exciting and rewarding endeavor.

Smell

A man writing about the sense of smell has related for us a joke which, though funny, is almost too true. He says "What bothers me is that the streets aren't safe, parks are dangerous, and the freeways are impossible, but under our arms we have complete protection."[6] We will talk later about this mania our society seems to have for anything that smells—at least anything which has a natural odor. In fact when we say "smell," the word itself has a negative connotation. This certainly is not true for the word *sight* or *sound* or even *touch.* Consider also how much worse you feel if someone says you smell as compared with telling you you need a shave or a haircut. That is, of course, unless they say you smell *good*, but the qualifying adjective is necessary if you are not to be offended.

In discussing the senses of smell and taste, several writers put them together and call them the chemical or the savor system. While, physiologically, this perhaps is accurate and although often we experience the two senses simultaneously, we do receive information through each of them and in many respects experience this information differently. Therefore, since we are trying to increase our awareness of the information supplied by our sense receptors, we will separate the two and talk first about smell and then taste.

As human beings our most basic and automatic urge is the urge to breathe. You may have experienced being at the bottom of a swimming pool and running completely out of breath. The feeling of *having* to get to the top is a very poignant one indeed.

All the air that passes through the nose, however, is not available to us for smell. It has been estimated that only about 2 percent of the air we inhale passes over the olfactory epithelium, a small patch of skin about the size of a dime, located in the upper back part of each nostril. When we really want to smell something, most of us sniff. This often works because sniffing sets up currents in the nostrils and forces more air over the olfactory epithelium and therefore more "smell molecules" reach these receptors.

There is probably more that we do not yet know about smell than do. We do know that the olfactoy stimulus must be both volatile and soluble—volatile to get into the air and into the nose, and soluble so that it can get through the liquid covering the olfactory epithelium. Some researchers now are suggesting that different parts of the olfactory epithelium may pick up different scents. But nobody seems to know exactly what happens after the stimuli are picked up and make contact with the receptor cells, except that then we can smell.

Of all the chemical elements there are, we can smell only seven: fluorine, chlorine, bromine, iodine, oxygen as ozone, phosphorus and arsenic. Given what we *can* smell, what we *do* smell may depend on characteristics of a particular stimulus. For example, how fast a particular odor stimulus is moving or how long it lasts may affect our sensitivity to it. Our odor receptors seem to adapt to a smell very quickly. Several days ago I visited a friend who had just finished scrubbing her bathroom floor. The smell in her apartment initially was so strong I thought for awhile I would faint! It did not take long, however, before I realized that I had become completely unaware of any unpleasant odor even though I am sure that another person just entering would have reacted exactly as I did initially. If you live in certain areas of the country, you may have experienced this same kind of phenomenon on days when air pollution was particularly bad. That first whiff of air in the morning can be almost unbearable. It is hard to know whether in this instance our quick adaptation to the smell is a blessing or a curse. Perhaps if we did not adapt so quickly, we all would be working harder to clean up our environment. On the other hand, this process is a blessing for many, a good example being a sanitation worker.

Along with all aspects of the sense of touch, smell could be our most pervasive sense. In order to see something, we need light; to hear something, we need a sound; and unless we are eating or drinking we often taste nothing at all. And yet, not only do we make very little use of this sense, but we do not even have an adequate vocabulary to describe what we do smell.[7] Things can smell good or bad.

They can also smell sweet, which is borrowed from the sense of taste and hot which is taken from our skin's sensation of temperature. In fact, often we describe the smell of something by saying that it "smells like" something else! Try thinking of all the words you use to describe smells. Chances are you won't end up with a very long list. It has even been suggested that we react to smells so violently at times *because* we do not have proper words to describe the smell. Certainly many of us react to a bad smell with a "pschooo!"—a drawn-up, wrinkled nose and a quick jerk of the head. That may be descriptive, but it is not very precise. Not only do we not have words to describe smells, but very rarely would we use odor terms to describe another person. For example, we might say someone was "sweet" or "bright," but how often would we say he or she was "fragrant"?[8]

The sense of smell does many things for us. What other sense organ can provide the stimulus for such clear, vivid memories of past experiences? Although we may not be able to tell from one moment to the next whether or not one color is exactly the same as the one we saw previously, years can elapse and a certain smell will still be instantly recognized. When I was a small child I used to have some kind of plastic in a tube which could be blown into all kinds of shapes and figures. Not long ago I was standing outside a specialty shop and got just a whiff of an odor which I immediately recognized as being the same plastic. Or think about the smell of a movie theater with its combination of people, air conditioning, and popcorn. Or the light or heavy fishy-salty smell of an ocean; a rain in the spring when the buds on the trees are just beginning to pop; smells which remind us of certain things because we all have certain things to be reminded of.

Compared with some other animals, we have a very weak sense of smell. Because of the society we live in, however, it is hard to know exactly how much we do use our noses. Think of the number of things we deodorize and then reodorize with another scent! We seem to dislike the smell of everything from our kitchens and bathrooms to every conceivable part of our body. We have specific sprays and liquids for hair, mouth, underarms, and feet, not to mention the curiously named "feminine hygiene" sprays and the masses of perfumes, colognes, lotions, and powders. We no longer simply open a window to air out a room; we spray it with Lysol, surround ourselves with eucalyptus leaves, and then burn incense. As one writer has suggested, it is possible that through either "propaganda or neglect" we could lose our sense of smell altogether,[9] and with the growing popularity of contact lenses, we do not even need noses to support our glasses![10]

Our obsession with "smell sanitation" is evident in many of the phrases we use to derogate those with whom we do not agree. For example, most of us have either used or heard such terms as "those stinking hippies," "male chauvinist pig," or "the rotten capitalists." You can probably think of more.

In light of all that we have said so far, it is interesting to note that each of us has a very particular natural body odor which has little to do with the many potions we dump on ourselves. Think about the person you most love. Do you identify a smell with her or him that is very specifically hers or his? If so, you probably love that smell and would recognize it anywhere just as our pets can recognize us regardless of what lotions we use on any particular day.

Not only do our noses give us our sense of smell, but they also react to other kinds of sensations. Some substances, like chlorine, can actually hurt the nose and others make it feel cool. Our nose experiences a substance like menthol as a temperature, a cooling sensation. In other words, the nose also has cutaneous sensations like the skin.

One writer has said that smellers are made, not born, by being taught which smells are good and which are bad. As small children, many natural scents, like the smell of human feces and sweat, were not unpleasant to us. And, since this is the case, it is possible to relearn how to smell and to develop more fully your own sense of smell as many drug dealers, perfumers, and wine merchants have done.[11]

Think for a moment about your own sense of smell. What do you smell right now? If your answer is "nothing," keep trying and see if you can detect anything you have been unaware of. When you think of "smelling," what images form in your mind? What are some of your favorite smells? your least liked? What odors from other people please you most? displease you most? Think about times when being able to smell has been most important to you. Pick up some very familiar objects around you and see if they have an odor. That most of the time we do not use our sense of smell very much does not mean we cannot become more in touch with the world around us, including other people, by improving our ability to smell.

Taste

The last sense which we will talk about is the sense of taste. As we said before, it is one of our body's two main channels of chemical information. By itself, the mouth is certainly our most important receptor because through it passes everything we need in order to live—food, liquid, and air.

As we all know, our sense of taste comes primarily from the taste buds, groups of cells with about one to two dozen cells in each bud. Children have taste buds scattered over the mouth and throat. By maturity, however, most of these cells, have died; only the ones on the tongue remain. As we continue to grow older, many of these cells wear out and die. Some are replaced and some are not. This process may help to explain why, over the years, food preferences may change a great deal. It is not hard to imagine, for example, how bad the spinach we hated as kids really might taste with the help of more taste buds!

As humans we can taste only four qualities: sweet, sour, salt, and bitter, and everything we taste is either one of these qualities or a combination of them. The taste buds are arranged on the tongue in such a way that we can taste only at the tip of the tongue, along the sides, and near the back or base. The taste buds in each location vary in their sensitivity to each of the four qualities we can taste; we taste sweetness best at the tip of the tongue, sourness along the edges away from the tip, bitterness closer to the back, and saltiness along the edges from the tip to the back.

You might try to experiment with different substances to see whether or not you can locate exactly where on your tongue you are most sensitive to the different qualities. This is not easy, of course, because in order to be tastable at all, a substance must be at least partially soluble in water, and it is not easy to keep a solution on one specific part of your tongue!

More than any other sense, taste is in many ways a combination of senses. Sight, sound, or smell can start salivation, which is the beginning of the tasting and eating process. You may have had the experience of seeing someone on television preparing food and realizing you were hungry and that your mouth was already "watering." Once in the mouth, the texture and temperature of a substance become important. I love tomatoes, but I cannot eat stewed tomatoes simply because of the way they feel in my mouth; and many people who love coffee and drink several cups a day cannot swallow one mouthful of iced coffee.

We usually lump together all these different sensations and call them *taste.* Nevertheless, no matter how something looks, smells, or feels, if it does not taste good, we will not eat it. In this way the action of our taste buds alone can be thought of as a separate sensory modality.

Although there are individual differences in taste because of age and the chemical make-up of saliva, most taste preferences, like several other senses we have talked about, are a result of cultural factors. In other words, how acceptable a certain food is to us has very little to do with the food itself but rather with whether or not anyone else in our culture eats it and whether or not we were ever given the substance as children. Can you think of anything which you eat and enjoy that your friends wouldn't even look at? When I was growing up in the Midwest one of my family's gustatory delights was boiled calves tongue. No one else I knew had ever even contemplated eating such a thing. Now that I am living on the east coast, I find that many people eat tongue prepared all different ways. Thus, when we speak of "cultural differences," we may be referring to many variations within any given culture.

We all know stories about strange things that people in other places eat. A person face to face in another culture with some revolting "delicacy" may ponder for several seconds whether to risk illness or rudeness. One woman writing about cultural food preferences has given the following comparisons:

> Thoughts of the stranger in North Africa offered the delicacy of sheep's eye, the South American Indians' communal consumption of drugs mixed with spittle, the Malaysian habit of eating raw meat stuffed into bamboo rods that have been inserted into earth and left for two years are singularly unappealing to Americans. Yet the typically American habits of eating corn on the cob, spreading masses of peanut butter on bread, or devouring watermelon on a summer day can evoke raised eyebrows from even the most cultured and traveled Europeans. A vast majority of the world's peoples would think a cheeseburger an astonishing concoction.[12]

Think about your own taste. What can you taste right now? Breathe in through your mouth, simultaneously rubbing your tongue across the roof of your mouth. Can you taste anything at all? If you are eating or drinking something, take a bite or sip and see whether or not you can isolate the exact second when you first taste the substance.

Blindfolded, try tasting several things which have a similar texture, like apples and onions, and see whether or not you can taste the difference. Now try it with your nose held shut. Some time ago several students in one of my classes and I discovered that there was no pleasure in smoking cigarettes when blindfolded. It seemed that when we could not see the smoke, we could not taste the cigarette.

Think about some of your favorite foods. Now think about your least favorite. Do either groups have anything in common? If you could have one thing to eat right now, what would it be? What would the flesh of another human being taste like, and how hungry would you have to be to try it? Think about your own eating habits. What do you usually do while you eat? Look at the food? Watch television? Read? Talk to other people?

Most of us pay very little attention to our sense of taste. We know when we like something and when we do not, but most of the time we let the food and drink we put into our mouths pass our sense of taste right by. How does your own body taste to you? How does the body of someone you love taste? Of all our senses many of us pay least attention to that of taste and therefore miss most of the information which comes to us from our world through our most important receptor.

CONCLUSION

We have talked about the ways we receive information from the world around us and from other people in that world. As we saw in the first chapter, Barnlund included in his Transactional Model of Communication many different kinds of cues which may be available in a communication situation.

In the interview we mentioned before, there were many public cues available to you: the office furnishings which you could see, the sound of a typewriter which you could hear, the odor in the office which you could smell, the thick pile of the carpet which you could feel as you walked to the chair. There also were several private cues which we have mentioned: the dryness of your mouth, your damp sweaty palms, the tightness of your throat. When your prospective boss entered, she provided you with many verbal and nonverbal behavioral cues, as you did for her, and like you, she had private cues of which you were unaware.

In any situation we probably are aware of only a small number of the potential cues available. We have not yet talked about how in various situations *meanings* are evolved. Hopefully, however, now you can begin to see that not only would different people be aware of different cues in a given situation, but they also might assign different meanings to the same cues, as we suggested earlier in talking about the "peace" poster on the wall.

In this chapter we have dealt with areas sometimes not thought of as being part of the study of communication. What we have been talking about, however, is *you* and your awareness of the things going on around and inside you. Communication is not all verbal nor is it just a combination of verbal and what most of us think of as nonverbal or body movement and touch.

Our everyday world is filled with sights, sounds, smells, and tastes of which we are often unaware. Learning to pay more attention to things we never noticed before can get us more in touch with ourselves and with others, and therefore in a better position to communicate effectively. For just one day try to *be* more in your world and see what kinds of differences it makes. Your body, *all* of your body, constantly is supplying you with information. All you need to do is pay attention to yourself.

NOTES

1. Lawrence K. Frank, "Tactile Communication," *Genetic Psychology Monographs* 56 (1957): 209–225.
2. Ashley Montagu, *Touching: The Human Significance of the Skin* (New York: Harper and Row, 1971), pp. 164–65.

3. Joan Steen Wilentz, *The Senses of Man* (New York: Thomas Y. Crowell Co., 1968), pp. 50–51.
4. Montagu, p. 125.
5. Ibid., p. 1.
6. Richard I. Doty, "The Role of Olfaction in Man: Sense or Nonsense?" in *Perception in Everyday Life*, ed. S. Howard Bartley (New York: Harper and Row, 1972), p. 146.
7. Roy Bedichek, *The Sense of Smell* (Garden City, N.Y.: Doubleday, 1960), p. 21.
8. Doty, p. 148.
9. Wilentz, p. 129.
10. Lorus Milne and Margery Milne, *The Senses of Animals and Men* (New York: Atheneum, 1962), p. 134.
11. Bedichek, p. 63.
12. Wilentz, pp. 150–51.

3 PERCEPTION

Such tricks hath strong imagination,
That, if it would but apprehend some joy,
It comprehends some bringer of that joy;
Or in the night, imagining some fear,
How easy is a bush supposed a bear?

Theseus in Shakespeare's *A Midsummer Night's Dream*, act 5, scene 1.

A Peanuts cartoon from several years ago pictures Lucy, Linus, and Charlie Brown lying on a hilltop looking at the clouds. Lucy congratulates Linus on his report of seeing a map of the Caribbean, a profile of a famous artist, and the major figures in a religious painting. After hearing this, a much-chagrined Charlie Brown decides it better not to report that what he saw in the clouds was "a duckie and a horsie." In their own ways both Shakespeare's Theseus and Schulz's Charlie Brown give us examples of how the perceptual process works.

Perception is a broad term and is used in many ways, but generally a study of perception is a study of how one's environment and the events occurring in it appear to a person. In the first chapter we discussed the fact that things do not seem the same to different people. We used the example of people watching a movie together and then disagreeing about what the movie meant. The problem is that things do not "mean"; people do.

In the second chapter we talked about all the different ways we receive information from the environment. Some of this information we pay attention to and some we ignore. What one person chooses to notice, another may completely disregard. And even if two people notice a certain thing or event, they may develop entirely different meanings for it. Perception, then, is the *development of meaning* as indicated in Barnlund's Transactional Model of Communication. Remember that in this model the arrows go out *from* the person as decoder *to* cues in her surroundings. The cues are not giving meanings to her but rather meanings are the result of a *transaction* between her and the cues she pays attention to. In other words, people create meaning in response to these cues so that they can "understand" events in the world.

SENSATION AND PERCEPTION

Sense organs receive stimulation. In the case of the eye, this energy is transformed into a pattern of nerve impulses to the brain. Through elaborate mental processes, these impulses become visual patterns in the brain, and one can *then* perceive objects. The stimuli reaching the eye cannot really be thought of as being "objects" until these processes occur. The same thing is true for other kinds of information we receive. Auditory stimuli are not really sounds until similar processes occur in the brain.

The objects we ultimately perceive are not exactly the same as those studied by a physicist. The energy impinging upon the sense organs of a woman and a dog are the same energy stimuli; however, what is "perceived" in each case is probably very different. Though perhaps not to the same extent, the same is true for two humans viewing an object.

When we talk about perception, therefore, we are not talking about what the physical world is made up of but rather what we as human beings perceive to be out there.

Perception may be thought of as being ". . . a dynamic searching for the best interpretation of the available data."[1] In other words, when confronted with an object or event, we try to develop what seems to us to be the best meaning for the happening. This process usually takes the form of comparing new patterns with familiar ones. Thus, our past experiences influence our later perceptions by building up for us expectations of what we will encounter. This process most often works to our advantage in that each time we come upon an object or event we do not have to start from scratch, as does a small child, in developing a meaning for it. Expectation, however, can lead to the development of an inaccurate meaning for a certain event and leave us very ill prepared to cope with the situation.

The important thing to remember is that we constantly are being bombarded with sensory stimulation. Some of the stimuli we isolate and attend to. What we give our attention to is determined largely by our past experiences with other events and by our current needs. Those stimuli for which we can develop no meaning usually go unnoticed. Our past experiences greatly affect our later perceptions. Since none of us has exactly the same past experiences, none of us has exactly the same perceptions of an object or event at any given moment. Thus, when you say to someone, "I can't possibly imagine how you see things that way!" you are quite right, since there is no way you can imagine all of his past experiences. What we can do, however, is discuss with one another exactly how we see things so that we can isolate the points on which our perceptions differ. And the sooner we realize that patterns are not in objects or events but rather their formations take place *in us*, the sooner we will be able to avoid disagreements about how something or someone *is* since we are really arguing about differences within our ourselves.

THE NATURE OF PERCEPTION

As we have said, when nerve impulses reach the brain, they are formed into patterns which give a person her perception of objects. When two people view the "same thing" and perceive different objects, this may be due to the different ways people pattern or organize what they see. We have all seen figures like those in figure 1, which can at one moment appear one way to us and at another moment appear entirely different.

Speaking generally, Gestalt theory would explain these alterations on the basis of a change in figure and ground. In Gestalt theory, *figure* is used to designate those things in the environment which a person pays most attention to or those things which one focuses on. *Ground* is used to designate all the other things which a person does not attend to at the moment. In other words, ground can be thought of as being all the things which become the background for the things (or *figures*) one does attend to. Imagine yourself going to a party where you know very few of the guests. When you enter the room where the party is going on, you

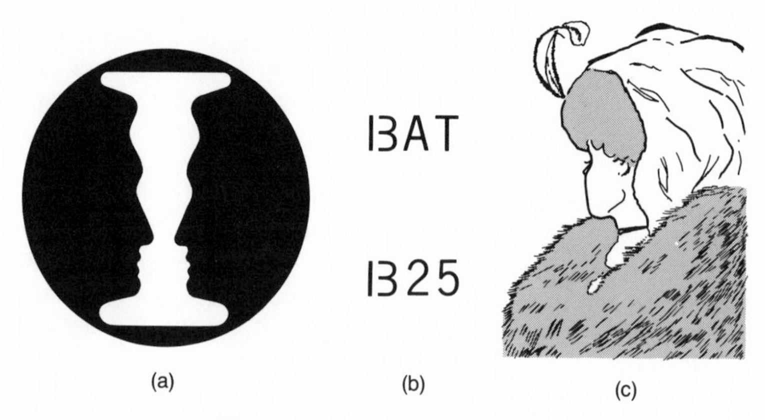

Figure 1. *What Do You See?*

probably would scan the crowd for one person you do know and focus on her. In a sense that person is for you the *figure,* and everything else in the room is the *ground.* It would be very difficult for you at that moment to say anything specific about other people or objects in the room until you begin also to focus on them. That is to say, in any situation, what is figure and what is ground can change depending upon where a person puts her attention.

Look again at (a) in figure 1. Here it is possible to perceive either a white vase (the figure) inside a black background (the ground) or two silhouettes facing each other across a white background. A similar kind of process helps to explain why people see very different things when viewing a painting, particularly, perhaps, a modern painting. Certain aspects of a painting may assume specific and important forms for one person, while another may see something completely different. In this case the two people simply would have organized or patterned the elements of a painting different ways.

There are many factors involved in the way a person will organize his perceptions at any given time. As we mentioned before, one of these is past experience; we tend to compare new objects or events with familiar ones. Another important factor is the person's needs at the moment. Using the vase and silhouette illustration in figure 1(a), if someone were given a bouquet of flowers and then shown this picture, she would be likely to see a white vase rather than the silhouettes. The same kind of thing occurs when we are looking for something specific in a drawer or closet. Often we do not really notice anything except the one item we need at the time. Recently I bought a piano and realized that I had no idea where to buy sheet music. While shopping the following day, it seemed that every other store I passed had a sign for sheet music in the window. Although I had passed these stores many times, I had never "seen" these signs before.

Although we have discussed past experience and needs of the moment as two different factors affecting a person's perception of an object or event, they often work together in helping to determine the way in which someone perceives a situation. For many years social psychologists have studied what they refer to as the human's need for *cognitive consistency.*[2] This term refers to our need to see things in our environment as being consistent with what we believe them to be. It is often used to explain why a person will change her attitude toward some element—a person, an object, or an issue—in her environment. For example, during the Watergate scandal many people were quite surprised and distressed to learn that some of the top leaders in our government had been involved in illegal activities. During this time opinion polls and editorials indicated that many people changed their attitudes toward those in government from something like "Our leaders know best," to "All politicians are crooked," or perhaps even more generally, "Everyone who has power is corrupt."

In other cases because it was difficult to deny the overwhelming factual evidence which eventually accumulated, many people decided that the "crimes" which had been committed were not really so bad, no one had really been hurt, and besides, all political parties engaged in such activity. These people just happened to get caught.

Cognitive-consistency theorists explain these positions as being the result of people's attempts to formulate attitudes consistent with their perceptions and with other previously held attitudes. In other words, if, before Watergate, a person thought that the President and his advisers were basically good men, following the revelations of wrongdoing he could have decided that since all politicians are crooked, it is not surprising that Richard Nixon and his men were, too. Or he could have decided that what these men did did not mean they were not basically good. In either case, his cognitions and attitudes became consistent or were in balance with each other. And in this way expectations based upon past experiences and needs of the moment can work together in affecting the way in which a person perceives any given event.

IMAGES OF FACT AND IMAGES OF VALUE

Based upon past experiences, we have what we might think of as an image of how things are in our world. This image is by no means a fixed picture which never changes; however, as can be seen from the examples above, we need to have the information we are receiving from our sense organs at any moment consistent with what we believe to be true about the world. In some cases this may mean that we will change an aspect of our image in some way to account for new and inconsistent information. An example of this kind of change would be the people described above who changed their view of politicians in order to account for the actions these men performed. At other times we may formulate our perceptions in some manner so that they are consistent with our image as did those people who did not perceive the President and his men as having done anything really wrong. Very simply this means that in cases like this we see what we expect and, therefore, want, to see. If any incoming information is not consistent with our image, we may ignore it or we may pattern or perceive it in such a way as to *make* it consistent with what we believe.

Let us look at this kind of process in a different way. If we take a long stick and put it down into a body of water, the stick will appear to be bent. Now, we "know" that, under normal circumstances, sticks do not bend when put into water. Therefore, even though the stick *appears* to be bent, we know that it is not. In the same way we know that the sides of the road really do not get closer and closer together as they recede into the distance even though they may appear to do so. We know this from past experience with roads, and we behave in accordance with our image of what roads do rather than how a particular road appears to us at a given moment.

In this way, as Kenneth Boulding has said, ". . . *Behavior depends on the image.*"[3] If you are beginning to understand this, then you are beginning to understand why different people can react very differently to the "same" stimulus. For each of them, it is *not* the same stimulus, since perception has to do with how we *experience* the world rather than with the world per se. In most cases a person's behavior will be logical to her, in other words, consistent with the image of the world she has.

It may be helpful to think of an image as having two different aspects: those of *fact* and those of *value.* For convenience, we will refer to these two aspects as images of fact and images of value, even though they are part of our total image of the world. Images of fact have to do with what we believe to be true about physical objects located in time and space. Such images are much more stimulus-bound than are images of value, even though, strictly speaking, images of fact may be faulty. In my mind I have an image of the island of Manhattan. In general, I know how the streets are laid out and where certain buildings and parks are in relation to one another. I know that at the southern tip of the island are two tall towers called the World Trade Center and even though I do not have as clear a picture of where it is as where my apartment building is, based on my image I could find it if I had to. These are images of fact. The streets and buildings in Manhattan are located in certain places and we could verify or correct our images if we wanted to take the time to do so.

Images of value are not easily verified, however, since they have to do with our *evaluation or rating* of a stimulus. In this way they are not as stimulus-bound as images of fact, but rather they come entirely from within us. Using again the example of my image of Manhattan, most people I know would agree that the World Trade Center is located at the southern tip of the island. Others may have a much clearer picture of where it is and what it looks like than I do, but we would probably be in substantial agreement about the facts. And if we did disagree, all we would need to do is go out and find it. I also think, however, that the two towers are hideous-looking and that their construction was a stupid mistake in urban planning. Now, although these evaluations are just as much a part of my total image of the towers as is their location, there is no way to verify that the buildings are indeed hideous or that their construction was a mistake. To a friend I could explain point by point why I think the buildings are ugly, and she could disagree with me on every point. How would we *prove* who was right? By going out to look at the towers? That might work, but probably what would happen is that we simply would find more points upon which to disagree! It would not even help to consult the most prestigious book on architecture. Even if the writer were to tell me that the buildings were beautiful, an architectural marvel, I still would think they were hideous.

Because of past experiences, people's images of fact can differ, and differ greatly. My image of where Iowa is in relation to other states and how large or small it is may be different from yours. In fact, we may have different images of the entire country because of how much each of us has traveled or studied. Because of these different images, suppose we were to have a disagreement about the location of Rhode Island. I do not know what you would do, but I would pull out an atlas. Now suppose I were to say "Ohio is a great state!" If you agree, everything is fine. What would you do if you disagree with me? Pull out your atlas?

Look again at figure 1(a) on page 50. Because each of us has seen vases and silhouettes, we probably can get one another to see both. Now suppose I say that the vase is a much more pleasing perception than the silhouettes. We are looking at the "same" stimulus and even though at one moment you may be seeing silhouettes while I am seeing a vase, we probably would not argue that only one image is there. We might argue for hours, however, about which of the two was the more pleasing.

Although we may disagree on matters which have to do with images of fact, most arguments among people are based upon differences having to do with images of value, and it is *very* difficult to prove anything one way or the other when images of value are involved. Both types of images are based upon past experience and therefore may differ greatly from one person to the next. But since images of value are not stimulus-bound, when we argue about them we really are arguing about ourselves. The next time you and a friend have a disagreement, try to decide which kind of image the argument is based upon.

CATEGORIZATION

A person's total image of the world is composed of the information he has received from past experience. This information may be thought of as being stored in categories, and each of us learns our category system from those around us. We do not come into the world with a series of categories waiting to be filled with information but rather we must be taught how to classify our world. Learning how to classify is facilitated by the use of language, and we will talk more about this in the next chapter.

Think again about our discussion of images of fact and of value. Our images of fact are composed of many categories, one of which permits us to perceive or classify a moving object with four wheels which transports people from place to place as a car or a truck or a bus. If we lived in a society without such things, we would not have an appropriate category and, if we did know about monsters, we might perceive a car as being a noisy, ferocious, foul-smelling monster. Until we learned a new category, the only way we could develop a meaning for the object would be to place it in one of the categories we did have—monster. If the stimulus were sufficiently ambiguous, we might ignore it. This, of course, would be difficult to do in the case of a noisy, moving car. The impossibility of ignoring many unfamiliar stimuli may help to explain the human's appeal to "the gods," magic, religion, or science.

In any given society most people will have similar categories. There will be big differences between people, however, on what things to put into what categories. And here we get into the problems caused by different images of value. Most of us have categories for "good art" and "bad art" or "good music" and "bad music." What specific art or music we assign to which category, however, will differ greatly. The same is true for perceiving, in other words, classifying, human behavior. We may agree that a certain person did a certain thing. In other words, because we have seen or read about this kind of behavior and have learned the same category for it, we can agree on what the person physically did. We may disagree violently, however, as to how the behavior should be evaluated. What is "moral" to me may be "immoral" to you. Taking this example further, we can see that not only may we put the "same things" into different categories, but our categories may not be the same size. I may have large categories of "moral" and "immoral" and therefore perceive much behavior along these lines. You may have learned to perceive behavior as being "helpful" or "harmful" and rarely even think about whether or not something is "moral."

The examples we have just given are related to our image of value. Since our values often are more important to us and much harder to change than our facts, when we evaluate behavior differently, we may be able to understand it only from *our* value category and therefore will not be able to discuss the act objectively because it is not the "same" act. A good example of this kind of situation occurs in the controversy over abortion. With sufficient medical and physiological knowledge, individuals from the two different factions in the controversy would agree on what the procedure is. This image of fact, however, becames very unimportant when one side categorizes it as "murder." Trying to prove that it is or is not murder is like trying to prove that the World Trade Center is or is not hideous! These two examples illustrate how difficult it is to resolve any differences of opinion when the people involved in the disagreement treat their values *as if* they are facts.

The example of differences of opinion on abortion points up another important factor in our process of perceiving and categorizing the world. Except for those adamantly opposed to the procedure, most people working against liberalizing the abortion laws would make an exception in those cases where the mother's life is threatened. In other words, how we classify a given object or event at any particular time has a great deal to do with the total context in which the object or event occurs. For example, many people would not define killing during wartime as "murder" because the total context—war—changes how they perceive and categorize this one aspect of a larger situation. Part of the total context in which an object or event occurs that might be easy to overlook includes our own needs at the moment. Most of us would classify certain behavior as "stealing." We probably would not agree, however, on which behaviors should be classified as "stealing-o.k." and "stealing-wrong." For some people *any* stealing may be wrong—any except that done on *their own* income tax, that is. And even for these people, if in a certain year they seem to have come out quite well and really do not need to "fudge" (new category!), stealing may become wrong *that* year for them. If however, the following year they are in strong disagreement with some of the policies of the government, then stealing at income tax time may become not only "stealing-o.k." but even a "moral act."

In summarizing how important the total context is upon the way in which a person perceives and categorizes a certain object or event at any given time, let us look at two studies which have been done in this area. In one study it was shown that if people were told a story about ships prior to seeing an ambiguous picture of a ship, they were much more likely to "see" a ship than were those who had not heard the story.[4] In another study the experimenters found that up to a certain point a person is more likely to perceive food-related objects in blurred pictures of household articles if he or she had not eaten for some time. At a certain point, however, apparently because of increasing hunger and frustration, the same person no longer "saw" so many objects related to food.[5]

You can perform a very simple experiment for yourself in order to see how important the total context may be upon how you perceive things. The next time you are near the top of a tall building, go to a window and look down. Try to judge the distance between you and the ground. When you are again on the ground, see if an equal distance horizontally feels the same to you as it did vertically.[6]

From these examples we can see that what a person perceives at any specific time is greatly affected by expectation based on past learning, by her needs of the moment, and, more generally, by the total context in which an object or event occurs. The two studies cited above illustrate certain of these factors: in the first, prior learning about ships may have created an expectation in the observers so that they saw ships; in the second, the observers' need for food affected the number of food-related articles they perceived. It is difficult to know for certain which of these effects is the stronger. In order to recognize something at all, one needs prior experience with it. On the other hand, what we perceive at any given moment may depend upon what we need to see, and if the need is strong enough, we may see things which, actually, are not in the environment at the time.

No mater which of these two factors is more important, however, the way in which we perceive and categorize an object or event can have a great effect on how we see the world and how we talk about this world with others. And remember that since we have *learned* our category system which makes up our total image of the world, just as other people have *learned* theirs, we often have very different images from one another, in addition to having very different needs at any one time. Because of all these differences between us and other people as to how we see the world, in a sense we can say that we all live in different worlds since we structure reality through our perception.

PERSON PERCEPTION

So far we have been talking about perception in general and why it is that different people may, very literally, see the same things differently. Your image of the world, in other words how you believe things to be, is very important in determining how you choose to live in the world. For most of us an important part of our world is other people, and how we interact with others is based to a large degree on how we perceive them.

In many ways the process of perceiving other people is similar to perceiving things other than people. In our discussion of object perception, we referred to the effect of expectation and needs upon our perceptions. In person perception these factors appear to be even more important than in object perception, at least as far as the sizes and shapes of people are concerned.

Albert Ames has conducted many studies using what he calls a distorted room.[7] The room, though actually distorted, is designed to appear as a regular square room when it is looked at with just one eye. When someone views the room in this way, another person either in the room or looking through one of its windows, will appear to be very distorted to the viewer, for example, will appear to be either very large or very small. Ames has found, however, that when someone looks at a person who is very important to her in this room, she is much less likely to see the person as being distorted. In another study, Warren Wittreich found that when people wore glasses designed to distort the image they saw, they were much less likely to see themselves as distorted than they were to see a stranger that way.

What does all this mean? First, we are very familiar

with the relative size and shape of people and therefore have a strong *expectation* for what we will see. Second, when people are very important to us, we may have a stronger *need* to see them as "normal." These two factors together may explain why we are unwilling to distort our image of at least some people no matter what type of experimental equipment is used.

Based upon these kinds of findings, it seems reasonable to say that how we perceive other people comes even more *from inside us* than does our perception of other aspects of our world. We have already seen that when we encounter objects or events in our world, how we perceive and classify them depends more on us than on the outside stimuli. This seems to be even more true when the stimuli are other people.

Think for a minute of the way we usually describe other people. Rarely do we mention *just* what we see. We may say they are dark or light skinned, 5′8″, 150 lbs., dark eyes, smiling, but we also usually add such things as friendly or unfriendly, happy, cold, and so forth. These kinds of terms do not tell what we *see* about another person. They describe what we *infer* about the other person based upon what we do see. We already know about the problems involved when we talk just about "seeing." I may not see the same things that you do. We may simply pay attention to different cues. Furthermore, I may not classify and evaluate the objects or events the same way that you do so that in a sense, as we have said, we are no longer talking about the same object.

In cases like this, however, we are not trying to infer anything about the needs, motives, or feelings of something. To use a previous example, just because I think the World Trade Center is hideous, I do not think it is malevolent. When it comes to perceiving others, however, we do make precisely these kinds of inferences.

When we observe the characteristics of a building or of a person, simultaneously with our perception we have certain feelings toward the stimuli. In person perception, however, the process does not end there. Based upon his characteristics and actions, we also perceive what feelings we *think* the other person is having. And this, obviously, we do not do with objects. If a book falls off a shelf and hits me on the head, I may be perturbed. I will not, however, try to decide why the book should *want* to fall off the shelf and hit me, which I would do if a person were to hit me with a book. Not only would I attempt to determine her motivation for hitting me, but I probably would go so far as to assign a certain trait to her. Based upon my past experience with people in general and with this specific person, I would say she was angry, crazy, wicked, violent, hostile . . . and how I reacted would depend more upon how I classified her than upon her original behavior. If I decide she's crazy, I may run away. If I decide she's angry, I may either hit back or try to talk to her. In either case my response is based upon her behavior, the total situation, but most important, upon my *perception of her motivation* or of her feelings. This perception depends upon the cues I pay attention to and the meanings I assign to them. Any other person in the "same" situation might see the behavior very differently and therefore react differently. This is a complex way of saying that, in this example, craziness is in the eye, or the head, of the beholder.

Think of all the information about another person which is available to us in any given situation. We may have whatever the other person specifically says about herself. We also have the total context that the person is in and the roles she chooses to play at the time. We may have a great deal of nonverbal information in the form of the person's bodily movements, gestures, tone of voice, clothes, and posture. From all of this potential information, we select certain clues to attend to and very largely ignore the rest. As we have said this selection is based upon past experience and current needs and therefore usually no two people will select the same cues since no two people have identical experiences or needs. Now again, based upon past experiences, we select certain cues from another and then, based upon these cues, we *infer* things about the person. If he is smiling, we infer he is happy. If he is crying, we infer he is sad. And our inferences are based upon what we have experienced and therefore what we expect. We have learned that when people cry, they usually are sad. When someone gets flushed and clenches his fists, he is angry.

STEREOTYPING

Not only do we make inferences like those given above and classify people accordingly, we also tend to associate certain categories or traits with other categories even if there are no relevant cues at the time. This, of course, is the basic process of *stereotyping.* When we isolate and attend to a certain cue from a person, we may infer that he has certain qualities or traits; in other words, that he is a certain kind of person. If we have previously associated people in this category with other characteristics, we may attribute these other characteristics to the new person also, even though we have not *observed* any such behavior. Perhaps the best example of stereotyping occurs when people come in contact with others from ethnic groups different from their own. The moment we learn that someone is from a certain group, we may, consciously or unconsciously, feel we know certain things about *him* because of the qualities we associate with other people in his "category."

By now it should be obvious why so often we have problems in interpersonal perception. In any situation, you and a friend may not isolate and attend to the same cues from another person. Because of differences in experiences and needs, you may infer very different things about another from the cues you do select, and associate your categories in different ways. Along with the inferences each of you makes, you may assign a label to the person. And not only may you assign different labels to another, you and your friend may have different meanings for or evaluations of the labels you do assign. Once each of you has assigned labels to another, you will assume that you have explained the person's past and present behavior. You also will have expectations for future behavior, which you probably will "see" since you expect to. And you will use the labels you have assigned to that person in describing him or her to another person. You will say, "She is lazy," "He is kind," "She is bright," "He is sensitive," and think you have said something about the person; what you really have done is describe *yourself* from the moment you first isolated a cue through your classification, inference, and labeling processes. Realizing that another observer might not see the same cues or develop the same meaning for them and therefore for the person should help caution against judging others and assuming reasons for a particular behavior. It also should help us to understand some of the problems we have in trying to communicate with others, particularly where there are big differences in past experiences. Many of the problems in communication between blacks and whites, women and men, children and parents, or between any groups or individuals may be based on the fact that in many ways we all live in different worlds and that, unlike what we usually think, there is no one "real" world.

CONCLUSION

In the preceding chapter we discussed all the different ways we receive information from the environment. In this chapter we have talked about how we develop meaning for this information, perhaps more accurately how we develop meaning for our sensations. While it is not absolutely necessary to have sensation in order to have perception, it is necessary to have information. A great deal of this "information" is inside one and has been collecting there from the moment of birth. Any new information encountered is compared with what is stored inside and, based on this comparison, a meaning is developed.

Previously, in discussing Barnlund's Transactional Model of Communication and the hypothetical interview, we pointed out some of the information available in that situation. We discussed some of the public cues, the private cues, and the verbal and nonverbal behavioral cues which might be noticed. We also said that it would be impossible for one to be aware of all the potential information in that, or any, situation; and now perhaps you can see why. Although our sense organs might be able to handle most of the information available, our mental processes are not able to work as fast as our senses because the development of meaning is much more complex than the registering of a sensation. And since in order to be fully aware of something we must be able to develop some sort of meaning for it, everything we think we know about the world comes to us, in a sense, secondhand. In other words, we do not experience the world directly but only through our perceptual processes. And because the elements in my perceptual framework are not the same as yours, we do not experience the same world.

Meanings begin in you as decoder in the communication process: in your particular selection of cues; in your particular categories; in your particular evaluations. What you believe to be true about yourself, other people, and the world, in other words, your images, are in your head.

NOTES

1. R. L. Gregory, *Eye and Brain* (New York: McGraw-Hill, 1966), p. 11.
2. For a good discussion of this topic, see Roger Brown, *Social Psychology* (New York: The Free Press, 1965), pp. 549–609.
3. Kenneth E. Boulding, *The Image* (Ann Arbor: University of Michigan Press, 1969), p. 6.

4. M. D. Vernon, *The Psychology of Perception*, 2d ed. (Baltimore: Penguin, 1971), p. 154.
5. Vernon, p. 179.
6. S. Howard Bartley, ed., *Perception in Everyday Life* (New York: Harper and Row, 1972), p. 7.
7. The findings reported in this paragraph are discussed by Hadley Cantril in "Perception and Interpersonal Relations," *American Journal of Psychiatry* 114 (1957), 119–26. For more detailed discussions of similar experiments see *Explorations in Transactional Psychology*, ed. Franklin P. Kilpatrick, (New York: New York University Press, 1961).

4 LANGUAGE

1st person:
How was the party?

2nd person:
Great! Really had a good time. John sure has fantastic friends.

3rd person:
What are you talking about?? It was a terrible party. In fact, I wouldn't even call it a party! It was more like a side-show! What a bunch of freaks John's friends are!!

How many times have you heard or engaged in conversations like this one? Most of us spend some time arguing with our friends about how good or bad something is or was. From our discussion on perception we can see that the people in the transaction above are arguing about images of value, how good or bad the party was, as well as about images of fact, whether or not it even was a party. The basic problem here has to do with the *meaning* each person developed for the evening and for other people involved, that is how each person categorized her perceptions of the event. How we categorize or classify events is greatly affected by the language we use, so let us see what language does for us.

WORDS AND MEANING

Language can be thought of as a system of symbols (words) that *stand for* other things (referents). There are many kinds of symbols. In the first chapter we said that the picture on the wall of the office was a symbol (). For some people, that symbol means "peace" and for others it means "victory." And even though one meaning may be newer than the other, neither is necessarily more "right" than the other. It depends on who is looking at the picture.

Think of all the different symbols you know, for example 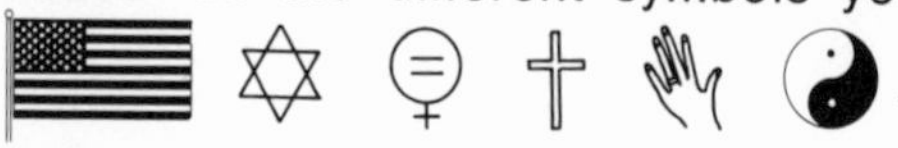 . What do each of these *mean* to you? How about all the different kinds of clothes or uniforms people wear: a nun's habit, a doctor's white jacket, a student's faded jeans and sloppy shirt, a cheerleader's pants or skirt and letter sweater, a policeman's helmet and heavy boots? How do you know whether a person is a student or a teacher? Think for a minute of all the different symbols with which you are familiar, in other words, all of the things which *for you* stand for something else.

One thing all symbols have in common is that the meaning of the symbol is not contained in it, but rather the interpretation or meaning is generated within the person looking at or displaying a symbol. This does not mean that many different people cannot have the "same" meaning for a certain symbol, but the meaning is in them rather than in the symbol. If *I* do not have a meaning for a symbol like  , it does not matter how long I look at the symbol, I will not be able to discover its meaning from staring at it. How would I learn what the symbol represents? Probably by asking someone to tell me what it means, and then the meaning would be *in my head* as well as in her head.

Take a moment now and look around the room in which you are sitting. Do you see a chair? What is the meaning of that chair? Obviously, it depends upon what one wants to do with it. Its meaning may be most often  or perhaps or may be  Now look away and say the word *chair.* The chair itself is localized in time and space across the room from you. Is the word or name for the object (chair) *in* the object across the room? Obviously, the word *chair* is not a physical part of the object chair. The word or name is in your head, or if spoken it is "in the air," or if written it is on paper. It is a *symbol* which *stands for* the object across the room from you. And as a symbol, the *meaning* for the word *chair* is in your head just as is the meaning for  .

As this example indicates, there are different kinds of symbols. Just as with the object chair, which can be symbolized as either  or *chair*, so too can a person be represented with the symbols *human being or*  . And again neither the symbols *human being* nor the symbol  *is* or is a part of the living creature who is being referred to. In each case, however, the *meaning* for the symbol is in the viewer's head rather than in the object being symbolized.

Suppose, for example, that someone says the words *human being* to a Frenchman. Those symbols may have no meaning for him; however, since he has had experience with the human being as an object and since he has learned another symbol for this object, he will understand, in other words, have a meaning for, *un être humain* as well as for  . Now suppose that some creature from outer space happens upon the drawing prepared by NASA (figure 1).

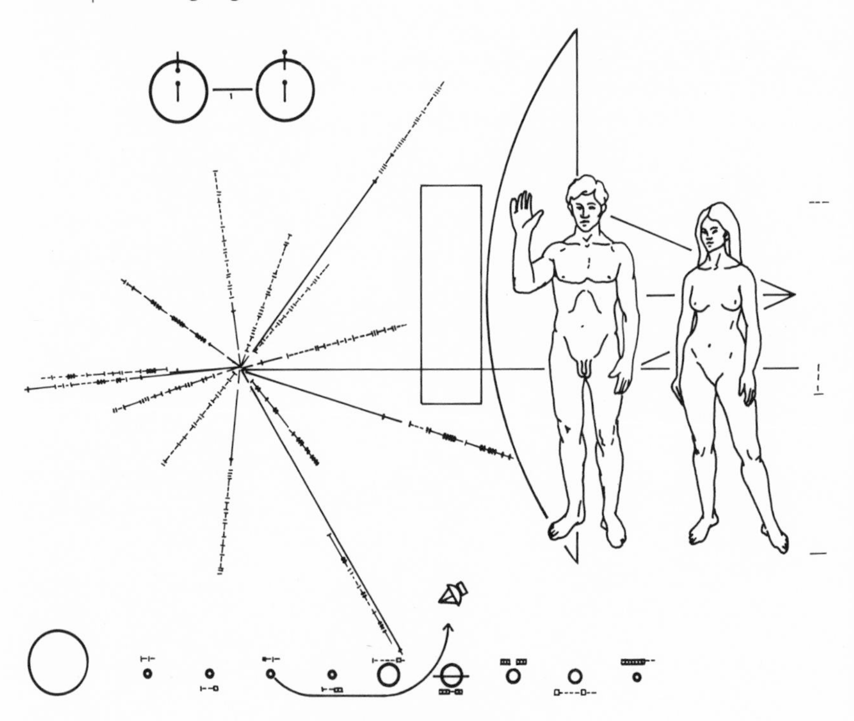

Figure 1. *NASA Drawing*

The symbols may have no meaning for the creature if it has never had any experience with objects that look like these symbols. As stated in the discussion on the nature of perception, the creature may not even *see* the symbol but rather connect all the lines in the drawing in an entirely different manner. That is to say, since the meaning of a symbol is not contained in the symbol nor in the object being symbolized—the referent—but rather in a person's head, any symbol used to represent a referent will be "meaningless" to a person lacking past experience with that referent. In other words, there will be no meaning *in him* for that symbol.

CATEGORIZATION

In chapter 2 we discussed the information from the world around us which is available to us through our sense receptors. In chapter 3 we saw that we develop an organization for this buzzing chaos through a process of perception and categorization. As a system, language greatly facilitates this process of categorization. How does this happen?

As children we may have been taught that the small, long-haired, four-legged animal that lived next door was called *dog.* With enough practice and reinforcement we soon learned to say "dog" when we saw that animal. We also learned that when we said "dog," our mothers knew what we meant even if the animal was not there at the time. What happened when on a later occasion we saw a huge four-legged animal with short bristly hair and heard it referred to as *dog*? We were probably just as confused at that point as when at another time we saw an even bigger four-legged creature with short bristly hair and said "dog," only

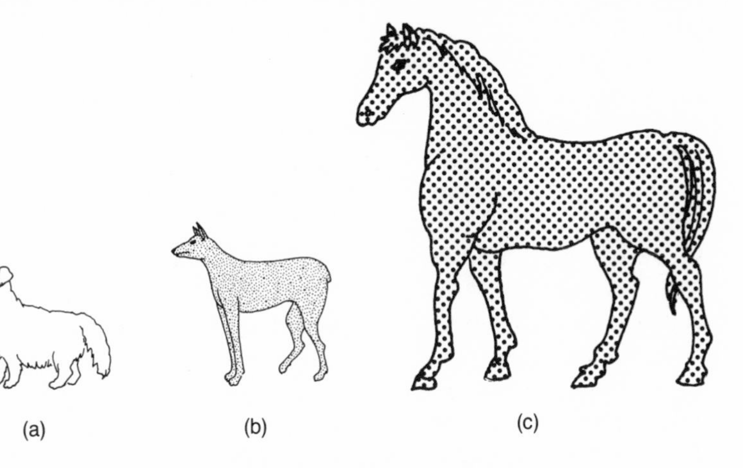

Figure 2. *Three Kinds of "Dogs"?*

to be told, "No, *horse*." In every case we were learning the name for a certain object; however, more generally we were learning the name for a category. In fact, every name, except, perhaps, proper names, is the name for a category. And when we name something, we actually are identifying it as a member of a certain category.

To categorize can be thought of as either overlooking similarities or overlooking differences. For example, take the categories *boot* and *shoe*. Specifically what makes a particular boot a boot rather than a shoe? Does it depend upon what it is used for? If so, when one wears shoes in the snow, do they become boots? Does the difference depend upon the thickness of the material used? Then how about vinyl boots as compared with wooden-soled shoes? In other words, what *attributes* are used as *criteria* for defining the difference between a boot and a shoe?[1] To put this a different way, in categorizing boots and shoes what similarities between the two are overlooked? What differences between various kinds of shoes are overlooked in the category *shoe*? In other words, how do we know when to call something a boot and when to call it a shoe? Since we all "know" the difference, this sounds very simple. For a small child just learning language, this sort of thing is not simple nor is it for us when we really try to specify the differences. As we said in the previous chapter, nothing is in any category until we put it in one. And since we learn our language from those around us, we learn our categories from them, too. If you doubt this, then try to imagine a child learning to categorize the world entirely on his own. What kinds of attributes would be most important for a child? Color? Movement? How successful would he be, living in a world where there were only "moving things" rather than "birds," "cars," or "kites?"

This example brings up another important point, the possibility of *multiple categorization*. Think of the many different ways in which a car can be categorized. It may indeed be a "moving object," or as we said in the previous chapter, it may be a "monster." Along with buses, airplanes, and trains, it also may be a "mode of transportation." And in addition to being in the category *car,* it may be referred to as being in the categories *used* or *two-door* or *Ford*. How we choose to categorize a particular object at any given time depends upon our past learning and experience and our needs of the moment. Since most of us have learned the category name *car* and have had experience with cars, we will generally agree that a given object is or is not a car. And if for some reason we need a more precise categorization, we also can agree that a particular car is either "used," a "two-door," a "Ford," or perhaps all three.

LEVEL OF ABSTRACTION

From this example it is apparent that one of the ways in which words in a language can differ is in their *level of abstraction.*[2] The level of abstraction of a word has to do with its generalizability or, alternately, with its specificity. If a word is very general, in other words, at a very high level of abstraction, it represents many different kinds of things; a word at a lower level of abstraction, however, stands for only a few or perhaps just one thing. For example, if I say to you "my car," and you are familiar with my car, you will be able to picture what I am talking about. This picturability, however, will decrease rapidly from "my car" to "car" to "vehicle" to "mode of transportation" to "moving object." An illustration of this concept is shown in Figure 3.

On each level of abstraction, as we gain in generalizability, we lose in specificity or picturability. The category *mode of transportation* allows us to discuss many things that "my car" does not allow us to discuss. We no longer can be sure, however, that what *I* mean by "mode of transportation" is what *you* mean by "mode of transportation"; that is not true when we talk about "my car." Therefore, even though we may use the same words or category

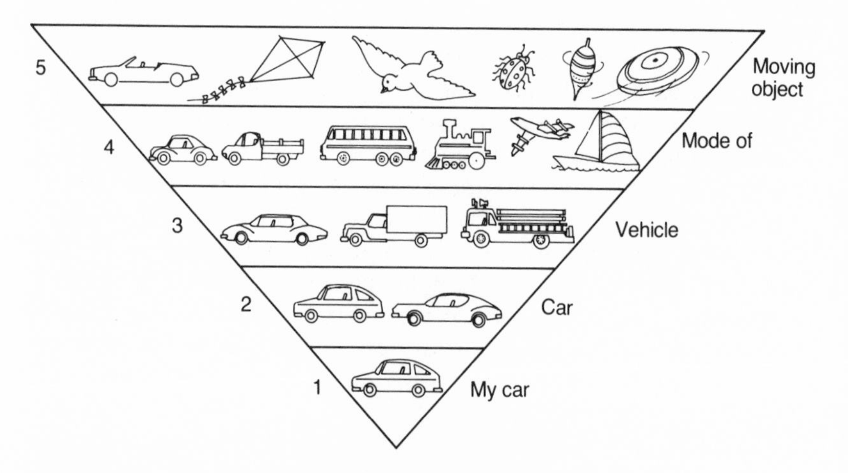

Figure 3. *Level of Abstraction*

names, as we go higher and higher in the level of abstraction, we cannot be sure that we are thinking of the same things when we use the same words. If someone says, "This country needs to streamline its modes of transportation" and another disagrees, it may be because the first person means its system of mass transportation and the second is thinking about trucks and trains for hauling cargo.

DEGREE OF ABSTRACTION

We have been talking about words as symbols. We have seen that the word, as a symbol, is not the object nor is it any part of the object being represented. We also have said that words are names of categories and that the level of abstraction of any word can affect the generalizability and picturability of a given word.

The words we have discussed so far have been words which represent or stand for concrete things in the world. Shoes, boots, and cars are concrete objects, and can be seen, touched, smelled, heard. All words are not like this, however. Words can differ not only in their level of abstraction, but also in their *degree of abstraction.* For example, take the word *boot.* Looking at Figure 4, you can see that although there is not a direct connection between the object *boot* and the symbol or word *boot*, there is a definite mental image for the referent class which corresponds to the physical object.

When we talk about boots, we will have different mental images of what we mean since we have abstracted from the category *boot* to a particular boot. This is a matter of mental selection and is based upon past learning. Since, however, all of us have had direct experience with the concrete object we are talking about, we probably will have a mental image sufficiently similar to continue our discussion.

But what happens when we begin a discussion which involves a word like *freedom*? (See figure 5.) Since there is no concrete referent in the real world for the word, there can be no "object category" as such. In other words, there is no way we could gather together in a box all the different kinds of "freedoms" in the world. And although doing so for boots would be a monumental (not to say

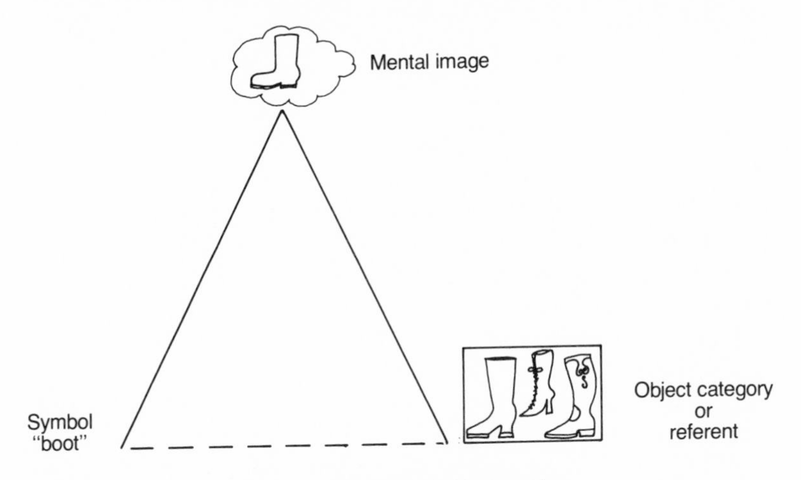

Figure 4. *Degree of Abstraction*

absurd) task, it would, theoretically, be possible.

Using a similar diagram, the problem with words like *freedom, justice,* or *communism* can be illustrated in two ways, as shown in figure 6. You can see that in (a) there can be no direct connection between the object category *freedom* and the mental image since there is no object category as such. In this case the right side of the partial triangle leads nowhere because there is nowhere to stop when one hits a "freedom." In (b) there may be a direct connection, but the referent in this case simply is all the life experiences any particular person has had, including experience with the word or symbol *freedom.* And since all of us have had different life experiences, there is no way that our "referent boxes" can be similar and therefore no way we can be sure we have in any way similar mental images when we use such a word. As a matter of fact, one interesting thing about words is the way in which, over time, meanings for certain words can change. In the case of the word *freedom,* it appears that for many people the word is coming more and

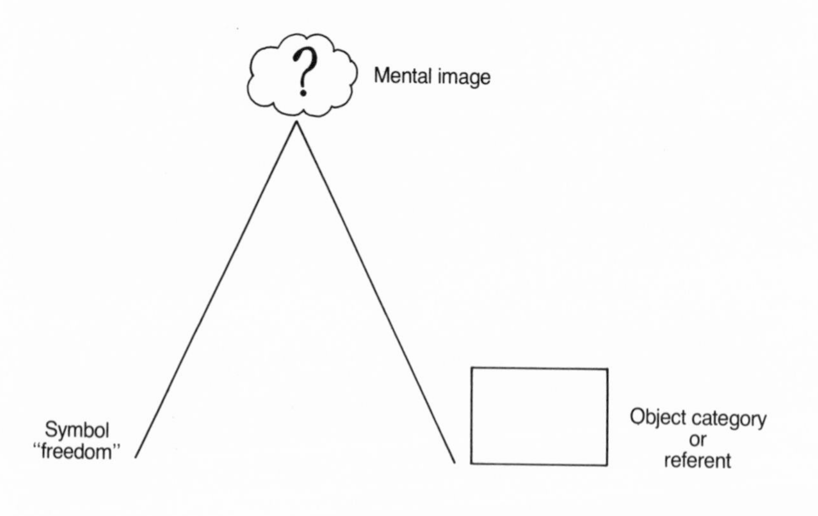

Figure 5

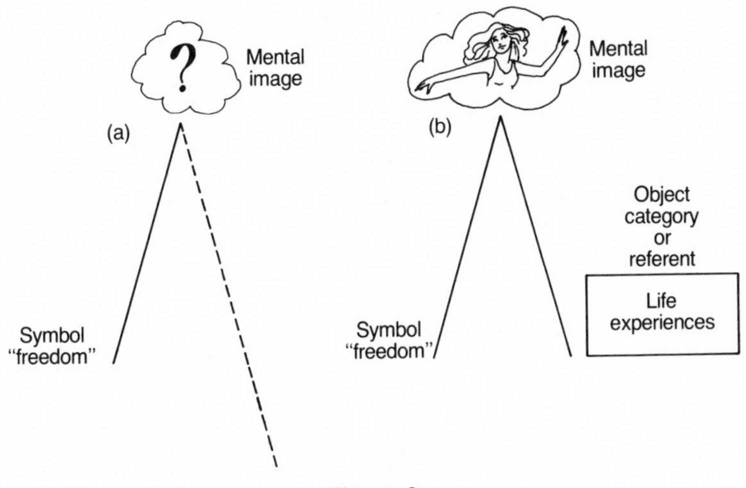

Figure 6

more to mean "freedom to . . ." rather than, as in the past, "freedom from. . . ."

LEVEL AND DEGREE COMBINED

By now it is apparent how abstract words can be. It also may be apparent that the more abstract the word, the more chance that any two people will not have the same mental image for the word and thus will disagree because in reality they are not talking about the same thing. Consider, for example, an argument between a young woman and her parents. In trying to explain her dissatisfaction, she may refer to her, or their, "lifestyle." Unless they have had such a discussion before, neither side may be entirely sure what they mean by *lifestyle,* let alone what the other side means. Based on our discussion of language, how would you suggest they begin to resolve their problem?

Look at figure 7. One problem with the word *lifestyle* is its *degree of abstraction*; in other words, there is no con-

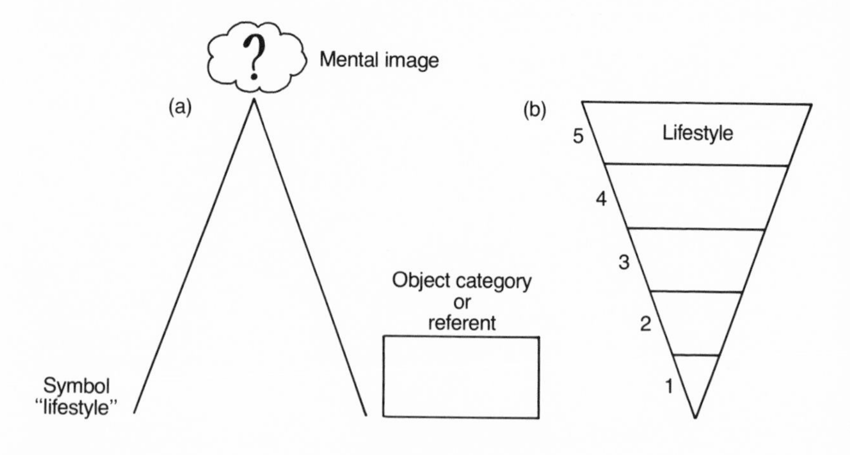

Figure 7

crete referent for the word and therefore almost no way in which the parents or the parents and their daughter can have similar mental images for this word, as depicted in (a). One way of trying to resolve the problem would be to make the word more concrete by moving down the pyramid of *levels of abstraction* (b). Examples of categories that might appear on these levels are illustrated in Figure 8.

This is, of course, not the only possible reduction, and as a matter of fact the daughter probably means more than simply wanting her own car. This is a start, however, and whereas her parents might have been most upset by her statement that she wanted to "change her lifestyle," they may or may not agree that she needs her own car. In either case, however, the problem has become more concrete for everyone. Whereas before her parents may have had all kinds of mental images about her desired new lifestyle, now they know she means she wants a car. And she no longer will be amazed by the doubts they have about her wanting to change her lifestyle when all she meant was that she wanted a car of her own.

Although the degree of abstraction and the level of

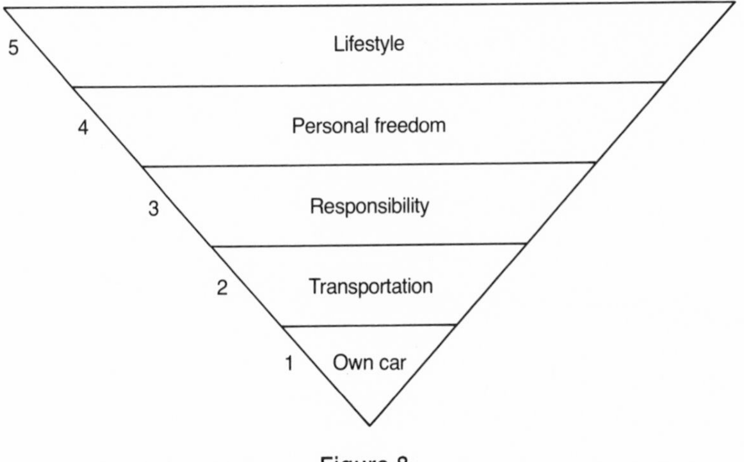

Figure 8

abstraction of a word are different, the two work together since all words are *symbols* and *names for categories.* In some cases there are obvious concrete referents for the category names or the words, and in some cases there are not. And especially when there are not, we need to be very careful that we understand what we and what another person means when using such words.

Decide for yourself what you mean by some of the following words. After all, that's where the meaning is.

education	health	dishonesty
freedom	democracy	justice
honesty	pride	religion
success	insanity	liberty
murder	cruelty	tyranny

THE BENEFITS OF LANGUAGE

Language as a system of words or symbols helps us in many ways. First, as symbols we can use words to stand for other things so that we can talk to each other about our homes without having to carry them around with us to point to when we want to refer to them. Imagine how difficult it would be to carry on a conversation with someone if we had no words and had to have all the objects we wanted to refer to close enough to us to be able to point to them. Second, language helps us in reducing the complexity of our environment since each word is really a category name and may include many nonlinguistic items which are similar in some ways and different in others. This means that each time you see a particular object you have not seen before, you do not need to learn what it is called. You know that this structure you see standing in front of you is called a *dorm* even though it does not look exactly like any other dorm you have seen before. Third, since language is a system of symbols which stand for *categories* of things, words allow us to communicate with one another on higher levels of abstraction than would be possible if we had to specify each particular item we wanted to include in our discussion. Thus, we discuss the problems of our "modes of transportation," or of the "military industrial complex," or of the "business community" and perhaps solve broader problems than we could if we had to talk about each particular item in each category. As we saw before, however, at this level of abstraction there may be problems until we *do* specify what we mean by each category.

There is yet a fourth way in which language can benefit us. And that is that words enable us to form expectations. Since words stand for categories of things, *repeatability* is possible. We know what to expect from a car because we know the attributes which are used as criteria in defining the category *car.* If we had no such category, each time we came in contact with a car we would have no idea what to expect from it since no two cars are exactly the same nor is any one car exactly the same from one time to the next. Perhaps we could agree to call a car something else, but in this case all we would be doing is changing the name of the category, not the category itself. As a matter of fact, changing the category name is easier than changing the items in the category. For example, if someone were to ask me to change the word *pound* to *blump*, I would wonder why, but I would still know what it was. When, however, I am asked to change my whole system of nonlinguistic and linguistic categories to *liters*, *meters*, and *grams*, I am going to have great difficulty in knowing what each one of them really is!

Although words enable us to form expectations, we must be alert to the process of expectation-formation based on language. For example, with our language we can categorize people in many different ways. Look at the following list of words. Figure out what expectations, if any, you have for a person who is described as being a member of each category.

businessman	Catholic	policeman
Jewish	black	Chinese
female	student	Protestant
white	male	Spanish
homosexual	upper class	social worker

Based upon past learning and experience, some categories may be more important for some people than for others. Your own sex, race, religion, social class, political affiliation, or profession may influence the way you categorize others. And depending upon the situation, some categories may be more useful and appropriate at some times than at others. The point is that since words allow us to categorize and form expectations, we may at times see only those things we expect to see and, as you may have realized from the list above, react to things and people based upon our expectations rather than the particular thing or person with us at the moment.

A good example of these principles in operation is demonstrated in a study performed by psychologist Roger Brown. In his study, Brown showed pictures of one man to a group of people. Each picture showed the man with a very different facial expression. To some groups of people Brown said that the pictures represented different emotions. To other groups he said that the pictures were of different men. When asked to describe the pictures, the first group talked about such things as smiles and frowns. The second group described differences in facial structures like the nose. In other words each group "saw" what Brown had led them to expect to see; the first group saw different emotional expressions and the second saw different men.[3]

You probably have realized that what we are talking about is a good description of one basis for prejudice against various groups of people. It is amazing, however, that for many of us prejudice and stereotyping often are based upon very little direct experience with individuals of a certain group. Most of what we think we know about a certain group comes to us through conversations with others or through reading—in other words, through words or symbols rather than through actual contact with the referent or person. And what is even more amazing is that words as producers of expectations are so powerful that a person can hold firmly to a prejudice, even though direct experience with members of a certain group is contrary to her expectations. Rather than revise the expectations, the person may say that Sam certainly isn't a typical ______.

In order to stop the very natural process of stereotyping, we need to remember that all items in a category are not exactly, or even in many cases remotely, the same. Alfred Korzybski has suggested that one way of remembering the nonsimilarity of items in a category is mentally to attach index numbers to each instance of a category.[4] For example, we have a category *female*; however, this does not mean that $female_1$ is the same as $female_2$ or $female_3$. More specifically, Jane, Cindy, and Helen are all "female," but each of them is very different from the other. Therefore, when we say that Helen is a female, what we have said is true, but so far as describing the particular qualities of *Helen,* we have said almost nothing.

HIDDEN MEANINGS

We have discussed how we use words to represent or stand for things. Words as names for categories can help us form expectations, but this process can also be a hindrance—as in the case of stereotyping.

A more subtle aspect, however, and one which we sometimes overlook, is that not only do we use words to *represent* things; we also use them to express our *attitudes* toward the things we are referring to. Look at the following pairs of words.

strong-willed/stubborn
overweight/piggish
single/spinster
forceful/overbearing
woman/broad
Italian/wop

As this list shows, we use words to symbolize nonlinguistic categories, but we also use slight variations of those words, "synonyms" if you will, to express our attitudes towards the item or items in those categories. In this sense, some words are much stronger than others and it often is possible to determine a person's attitude by listening to the words he or she selects.

Since words are used to reflect attitudes, they can be used also to mold attitudes. During the past few years we have seen this process in operation several times. During the war in Viet Nam, we constantly heard terms such as "peace with honor," a "just peace," and "protective reaction strike." Later, in the midst of the "Watergate affair," we heard about "executive privilege" and "gaps" on tapes; only later did these become "erasures." Another example was the "energy crisis." The word applied to a particular situation can affect how we react to it. Apparently those in charge thought we would react differently to an energy "crisis" than to an energy "problem" or "shortage."

The above examples certainly are not isolated incidents. All of us use this process every day of our lives. In fact, would you say now that you are being "educated" or "indoctrinated"? Is what you read "information" or "propaganda"? And what determines which of these categories is "right"? The intent of those instructing you, or your attitude toward them and their ideas?

The point is that the way we categorize our world determines how we react to or live in it. As we have seen, language greatly facilitates this categorization process. Therefore, our reactions to our world significantly are based upon language or the words we use. Since there are so many different ways of classifying or naming the events going on around us, it may be a futile question to ask what the "best" ways are. Earlier, however, we said that one of the benefits of categorization is *prediction.* Therefore, for any person the "best" categorizations are those which are the most accurately predictive. The categories and names we learn as children are not necessarily the most accurately predictive for us as we grow older and as our society and our world change. Perhaps the people you feel are most successful in living in their world are those who are most flexible in recategorizing and renaming the events going on around them.

As a system of symbols representing the nonlinguistic world, language can be thought of as being similar to a map of a territory.[5] Since we are all familiar with maps, we know that the best maps are those which represent most accurately the given territory. As we learn more and more about a territory, maps can and should change in order to reflect new information. To hold on to an old map in such a case would be foolish. This is precisely, however, what many people seem to do with language. We now know that all communists are not banded together as agents of the devil. Some people, however, still refer to the "red menace."

We now know that all women do not want to be soft, passive, and unprofessional, nor do all men want to be hard, aggressive, and "on top of things." Some people, however, still refer to qualities like these as "feminine" and "masculine." In such cases, the people involved have not looked at the territory nor redrawn the map and therefore are not prepared to deal in a precise way with the changing world around them.

In most cases we categorize and name things as we want them to be. We also change categories and names when expedient. A good example of this is the current controversy over Sunday "blue laws." If in a given city drug stores can be open but grocery stores cannot, it may be necessary to recategorize and rename certain "grocery stores." In this case we would have changed the attributes used as criteria for defining a particular category; any store selling family medical supplies, for example, bandaids, might become a "drug store."

If you can understand this example, then you realize that reality is to us whatever we say it is, thus determining our attitudes and behavior toward it.

TRANSACTIONAL MODEL OF COMMUNICATION

Let us look again at Barnlund's Transactional Model of Communication. The arrows going out from each communicator indicate that the meaning is going *from* the person *to* the cue. This development of or assignment of meaning by the person is obvious when we talk about things such as the poster on the wall of the office described in chapter 1.

In verbal communication the process is the same. The words we exchange with one another do not *have* meaning; *we* have meaning *for* them. The meaning of the word is inside us rather than in the word. In the model, person 1 says something to person 2 ($\mathbf{C}_{BEHV}$); in other words, she encodes, or puts into words, an idea she wants the other

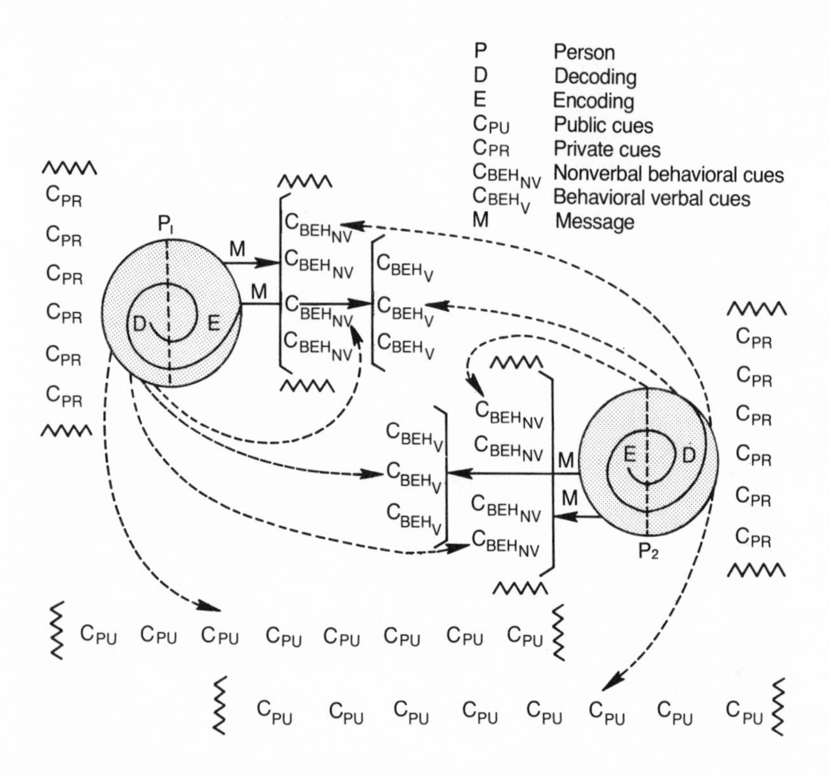

Figure 9. *The Transactional Model of Communication*

person to receive. Person 1 uses words to which she applies a certain meaning. If person 2 pays attention to person 1, he will decode the message; in other words, he will take the words and assign his own meaning. Whether or not both people now have the same idea depends upon how similar their meanings are for the words used. If we are talking about boots and chairs, we probably will have meanings for these words which are sufficiently similar to continue our discussion with no trouble. When, however, we deal with words such as freedom or lifestyle, we may have problems and disagreements because we simply may not mean the same things when we use these words.

As Barnlund has said, "Communication describes the evolution of meaning." This does not necessarily mean that when we communicate we "evolve agreement," but that when we communicate with one another on a verbal level, we are developing meanings between us and understanding more about what we and the other person *mean* when we use words.

NOTES

1. For a complete discussion of criterial attributes, see Roger Brown, *Words and Things* (New York: The Free Press, 1958).
2. For an interesting discussion of the various levels of abstraction of words, see S. I. Hayakawa, *Language in Thought and Action* (New York: Harcourt, Brace & Co., 1941).
3. Brown, p. 219.
4. Alfred Korzybski, *Science and Sanity* (Lakeville, Conn.: The International Non-Aristotelian Library Publishing Co., 1933).
5. Korzybski, p. 58.

5 NONVERBAL COMMUNICATION

> The lawyers' office is on a small, quiet street. Marianne gives her husband a peck on the cheek and gets out of the car. Johan waves to her and drives off. It's raining heavily and Marianne hurries into the doorway and up the stairs of the dignified old house with its gleaming bannisters, stained-glass staircase windows, and heavy marble walls. She nods to the secretary and the day's first client, who is already sitting waiting. Once inside her room she changes her shoes, hangs up her jacket, and puts on a sweater. She asks the client to come in.
>
> From Ingmar Bergman's *Scenes From a Marriage.*

In chapter 2 we dealt with the channels through which messages can be sent. Information can be received from another person through eyes, ears, nose, mouth, and skin. In addition to all the information available from other people, one also can receive cues from the environment, as demonstrated in the discussion of Barnlund's Transactional Model of Communication in chapter 1.

In the passage above we can see that there is a great deal of information available to the people involved in the scene. They may select cues from the "small, quiet street" or from the "dignified old house" and evolve various meanings for them. So far as the communication between the people is concerned, only a very small portion is verbal. In other words, in only a small part of their total interpersonal communication do they utilize language. (In the final sentence of the passage, we assume that Marianne used words in asking the client to come in, although even here she could simply have motioned to the client.)

But look at all the other ways the people involved exchange messages: "Marianne gives her husband a peck on the cheek"; "Johan waves"; "She nods to the secretary and the day's first client." All of these ways of receiving information without the use of language is known as nonverbal communication. In this chapter we will look at three aspects of the very large field of nonverbal communication.

The first is the environmental, specifically, the various uses of space. Second, we will explore various bodily aspects of nonverbal communication. And finally, we will discuss paralinguistics, which falls between verbal and nonverbal communication. First, let us look at environmental factors as one aspect of nonverbal communication.

ENVIRONMENTAL FACTORS: THE USES OF SPACE

If you were to enter your own room for the first time, what would it tell you about the person who lives there? How is the furniture placed? How can people sit in the room? Close to one another? Far away? Facing each other? Side by side? Are there tables, lamps, footstools, which would separate one person from another?

For example, look at the diagrams of two different living rooms shown in figure 1. In the first room, we can see that unless two or more people sit side by side on the couch, something, or some things, will be separating them. In the second room, everyone will have a direct line of contact with everyone else. Compare the houses, rooms, or apartments of people you know. Are there some places where you are more comfortable than others? These differences, obviously, have a great deal to do with the other people and your relationship with them, but try to decide whether or not the physical arrangements of the rooms also have an affect on you.

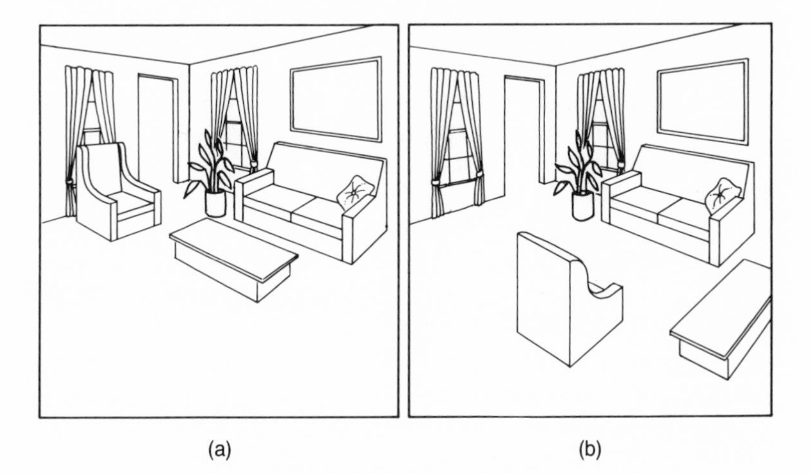

(a) (b)

Figure 1. *A Use of Space*

What we are talking about here is the use of space. The study of how people use space is called *proxemics* and includes both the use of environmental space and that of personal space—the actual distances we establish between ourselves and others.

THE FEATURES OF SPACE

In discussing these different aspects of proxemics, Edward Hall refers to *fixed-feature, semifixed-feature,* and *informal space.*[1] We will discuss the first two of these together and then look at the third.

Fixed and Semifixed Space

Fixed-feature space is space organized by permanent or unmovable boundaries like the walls of a room and the doors and windows in that room. Semifixed-feature space is that which is organized by objects within the fixed boundaries of that space. Look again at the two diagrams of a livingroom. The fixed-feature space remains the same in both pictures but the semifixed changes a great deal.

In many cases people consciously or unconsciously assign meaning to both the fixed and semifixed-features of space and respond accordingly. For example, the office of the president of your school probably is very different from that of one of your instructors. The president's may be located on the top floor of the major administration building and it may be very spacious with many windows. Often a large office located on a high floor gives the feeling that the person is important. If so, we probably will not just walk in as we might do in a small office located on a lower floor. These are examples of how people may assign meaning to the fixed-features of space.

Look at the diagrams of two different offices in figure 2. Suppose the diagrams represent the offices of two instructors whom you have not yet had for a class. How might you feel upon entering these two offices? If you think you might respond differently simply because of the location and placement of the desk and chairs, then you would be responding to the semifixed features of space in the offices.

From the two diagrams, we can see that distance between people and placement of objects may affect the

(a) (b)

Figure 2. *Semifixed Space*

interaction in a particular setting. There are many ways of looking at these two aspects. One is to examine the direction the people are facing. Sometimes the objects within a setting are arranged so that people will be facing one another, thereby encouraging interpersonal communication. This type of environment is called *sociopetal.* When the arrangement of objects in an environment discourages or prohibits face-to-face contact between people, it is called *sociofugal.* Sociopetality and sociofugality are determined by observing the *axis* or the body orientations of the people in a given setting. Figure 3 illustrates this dimension of space. An example of sociopetal positioning is represented in (a), whereas (b) depicts a sociofugal arrangement.

There are some environments which seem to have been designed to increase the sociofugality of the setting.

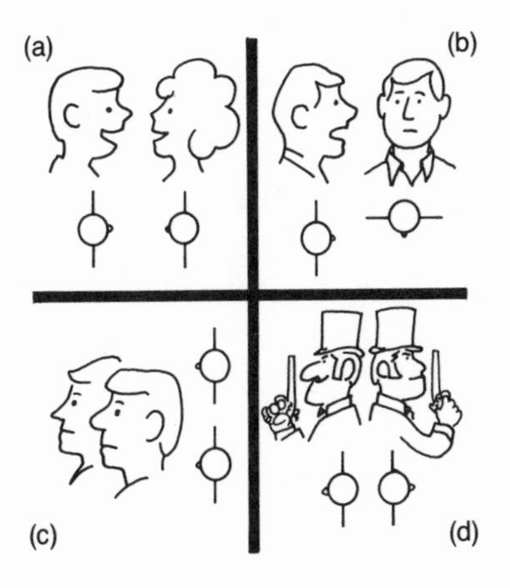

Figure 3. *Interpersonal Orientations*
The orientation of two communicators can be described in terms of "axis"—the positioning of bodies. Illustration (a) represents face-to-face interaction; (b) shows a 90° positioning; (c) demonstrates a shoulder-to-shoulder relationship. And (d) illustrates a back-to-back stance.

For example, some of the newer and more modern airports have waiting areas that look something like the one depicted in figure 4. (The squares represent chairs and the circles represent tables.)

In a setting such as the one in figure 4, it is difficult for a person to initiate a conversation with someone sitting in another seat. Any two people are sitting back to back (**1** and **2**), in which case interaction is almost impossible, at 90° angles to one another (**2** and **4**), or side by side (**5** and **6**). In the latter two positions not only can visual contact easily be avoided but in this particular case, there is a table between the people. In the one case where two people would be facing each other without an object separating

Figure 4. *A Sociofugal Setting*

them (**2** and **5**), the distance between them is too great to enable interaction to begin or to proceed easily.

In this setting, as in many others, the positions of the people must remain fixed because the seats either are too heavy to move or are bolted to the floor. In some settings, however, even if it is possible to change the seat positions, people usually will not do so for one reason or another. Rather, they may select a seat in a location and position which is most comfortable for them.

Look at the illustrations in figure 5. If two people entered a restaurant and had their choice of the various seating arrangements, they might sit in the booth (a) if they preferred to sit side by side or at the round table (b), which is not quite like the side-by-side in the booth nor the 90° position of the square table (c).

It is important to note that with any specific aspect of nonverbal communication, we are not so interested in what a certain feature, behavior, or activity means as we are in trying to discover how it influences the interaction between or among people. In this discussion of the use of space, we are less interested in why things were arranged in a given way than we are in trying to learn how that arrangement affects a subsequent interaction. By concentrating on the effects of spatial features, we *may* be able to arrange a setting in which communication can be facilitated, or hindered if that is the goal.

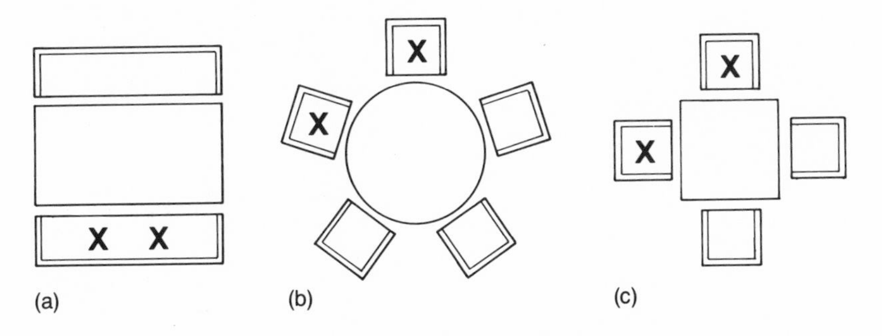

Figure 5. *Various Seating Arrangements*

For example, from what has been said so far, which of the classroom arrangements shown in figure 6 might lead to more interaction among the students, and why?

In studying fixed and semifixed-features of space, we have discussed the size and the location of a setting, the placement of objects within the setting, and the factors determining the position of people within the setting. Now let us look at the third feature of space which deals specifically with individuals.

Informal Space

Unlike fixed and semifixed-feature space, informal space travels with a person. It can be thought of as personal space or a personal "bubble" surrounding the person which changes from situation to situation depending upon the kind of interaction.

Edward Hall has studied the way people use space, emphasizing the possible breakdowns in communication between people of different cultures because of the different ways they utilize their personal space. He gives an example of a Latin American and a North American in conversation. During the entire encounter, the Latin American attempts

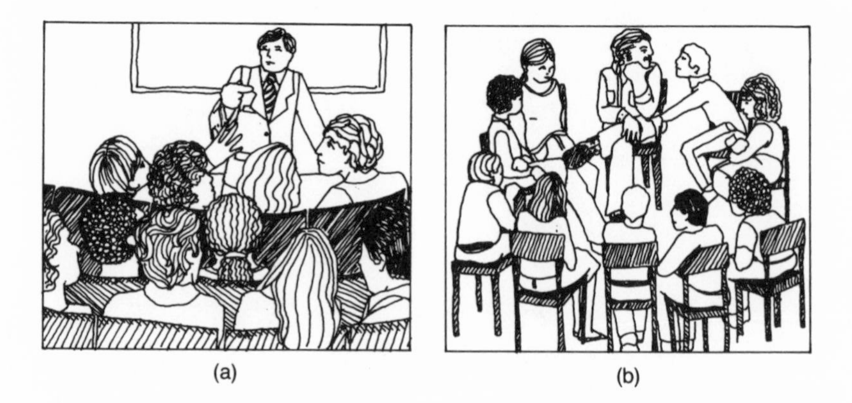

(a) (b)

Figure 6. *Two Different Classrooms*

to stand closer and closer to the North American who, just as slowly, backs away. Hall explains that at the end of the conversation, the Latin American will go away feeling that the North American seemed cold and aloof while the North American thinks to himself how pushy and forward those Latin Americans are!

Hall has found that across cultures, people tend to use specific distances for specific types of interactions. Look at figure 7. If you grew up in the United States, Hall says that you use the distances indicated for the types of interactions described alongside each distance.

1. *Very close* (3 in. to 6 in.)	Soft whisper; top secret
2. *Close* (8 in. to 12 in.)	Audible whisper; very confidential
3. *Near* (12 in. to 20 in.)	Indoors, soft voice; outdoors, full voice; confidential
4. *Neutral* (20 in. 36 in.)	Soft voice, low volume; personal subject matter
5. *Neutral* (4½ ft. to 5 ft.)	Full voice; information of nonpersonal matter
6. *Public Distance* (5½ ft. to 8 ft.)	Full voice with slight overloudness; public information for others to hear
7. *Across the room* (8 ft. to 20 ft.)	Loud voice; talking to a group
8. *Stretching the limits of distance*	20 ft. to 24 ft. indoors; up to 100 ft. outdoors; hailing distance, departures

Figure 7. *The Relation of Space and Interaction*

You can test Hall's theory by noticing the distances you use when interacting with others. The next time you speak with someone, check how close you are standing to each other. What are you talking about? You can even have some fun by changing the distance between you and the other person and then noticing how this change affects the situation; for example, how do you feel? Does the other person react physically? Does the topic of conversation change abruptly, or the tone of voice either of you is using?

The distances Hall gives are generalizations, as evident from the range within each specific distance. This means that although people from the same culture tend to use certain distances for particular kinds of interactions, there are individual differences within the culture.

Summary

The use of space is one kind of nonverbal communication. The way people organize their environment, and themselves in relation to others, affects the total interaction since the people involved will select certain spatial cues and evolve meanings for them. In this way, as Hall says, the use of space is a "silent message."

BODILY FACTORS

In discussing the use of space, we talked about both long-lasting aspects such as the placement of furniture, and about changing conditions such as one's position in relation to someone else. In other words, during any encounter between people, the location of the furniture is not likely to change, but the distance between people can change continually.

In discussing bodily forms of nonverbal communication, we can make a similar distinction. During the course of any single encounter, and even to a degree over time, we do not expect the total physical appearance of someone we are with to change radically. We are not surprised, however, if that person does change his or her bodily position, and we are even less surprised if the facial expression changes. Generally, then, bodily forms of nonverbal communication can be divided into *physical characteristics, body movements,* and *facial expressions.*

Physical Characteristics

When you meet a new person, what kinds of things do you notice first? Most people pay considerable attention to another's physical appearance, learning a lot from this alone. For example, one can usually tell a person's sex, approximate age, and relative height and weight. We might not agree on which *labels* to assign—if you are 6′4″ and I am 5′4″, you might say that a person 5′8″ is "relatively short" and I might say she is "relatively tall"—but we could probably agree that the person is around 5′8″.

In the discussion of perception in chapter 3, we said that we tend to notice those things which are most important to us. Look at the pictures in figure 8 and imagine yourself in these situations: you are a young black woman; you need directions to the campus library and spot the group of people shown in (a); you are a young man eating lunch at a table next to the group in the college Union (b), and you want to find out where the bookstore is. Which of the people in each picture would you tend to notice first, and specifically what about them?

We are dealing here with stable physical features, and they are important because a viewer or receiver may assign some importance to them. These features, however, are more or less *out of the control* of the person being observed. That someone appears to be a woman may give us important information; however, that in itself does not tell us very much about *what kind* of woman she is. Since other aspects of her physical appearance, like her clothing, hairstyle, and make-up, *are* under her control, we may assume that these kinds of things will tell something about *her*. Look again

Figure 8. *Stable and Changing Physical Features*

at the pictures in Figure 8. In (a) if you approach the young woman in the center of the picture, will she be friendly? Is she "with it" or "behind the times"? What else do you think you know about her? Now look at (b). If you approach the man seated on the left, will he be friendly? Is he a student or a professor? What else do you think you know about him? What do you think you know about the woman sitting next to him? What, in addition to the more fixed characteristics like sex, age, height, weight, do you think you know about these people?

As this example illustrates, we make inferences about people from their physical appearance. In many cases we may be wrong. But, we may be correct when we deal with people from our own culture because we have learned the cues that convey more or less the same types of information about ourselves. More important, however, is how each observer *evaluates* these cues. Look again at the pictures in figure 8. Can you distinguish between *what* you think you know about each person and *how* you evaluate these things? Physical characteristics, as nonverbal cues, are most important, then, for the meanings we assign to them, and for the ways in which our evaluations influence how we approach and relate to those around us.

Body Movements

As a form of nonverbal communication, body movements include such things as posture and position; gross body movements such as walking; arm and hand gestures; and head movements. Again, in dealing with this area of nonverbal communication, we are interested primarily in the *message value* of the movements—in the *meaning* observers assign to the movements and its effect on the communication between people, rather than the intention of the person engaged in the behavior.

Look at the group of pictures in figure 9. What would you say about each person?

As you can see, we put great significance on the way a

Figure 9. *Body Posture and Body Movement*
(a) Above: Do you think this woman is tense or relaxed? If you did not know her, how would you feel approaching her to ask a question? Why?
(b) Top right: Does the man in the center of this picture seem to be in a hurry? How do you know that? Would you describe the man behind him as being in a different frame of mind from the first man? Why or why not? Which of the two men would you feel more comfortable in approaching to ask a question? Why?
(c) Bottom right: What would you guess is going on between these two people? Which person seems to be more willing to discuss the topic of conversation?

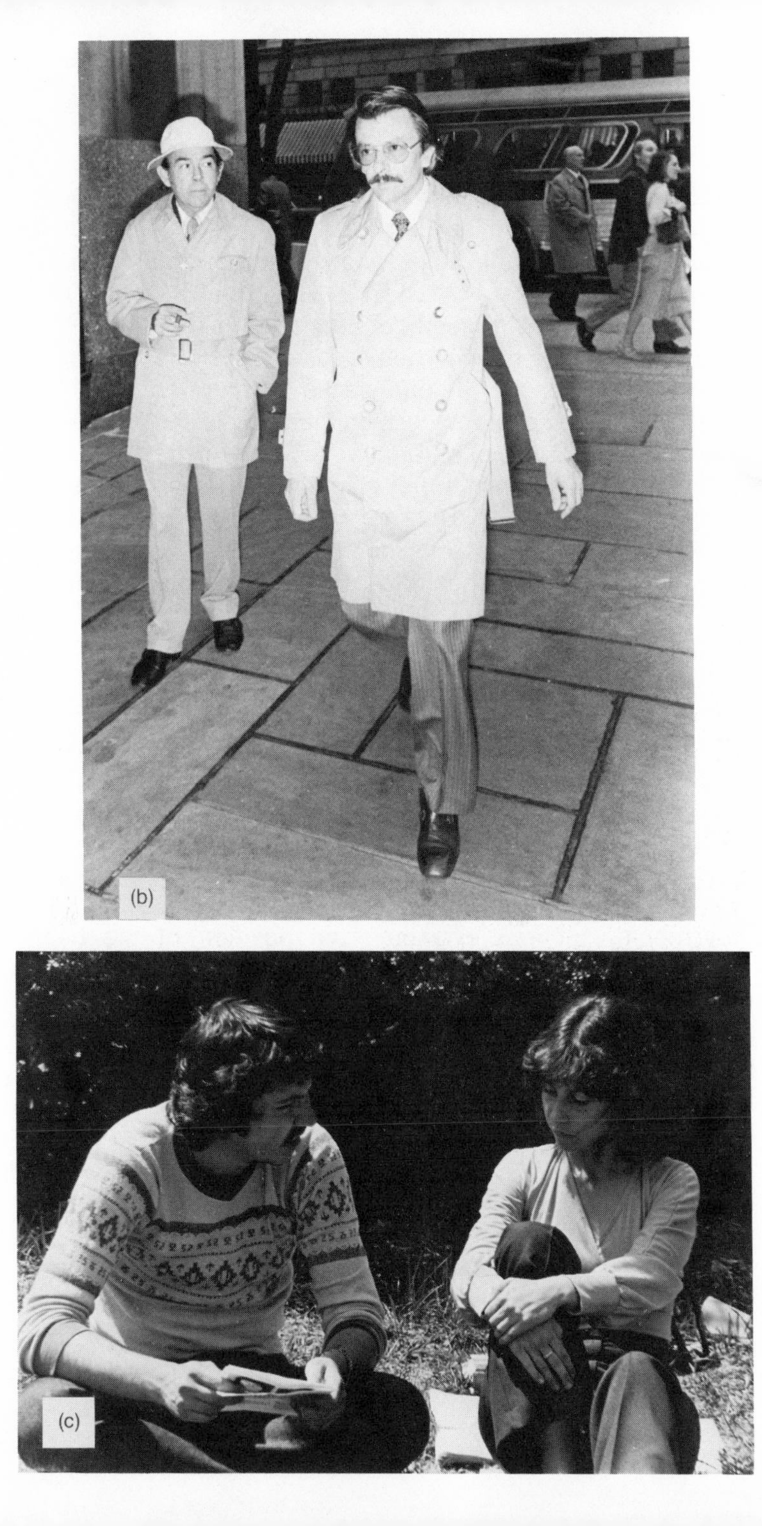
(b)
(c)

person holds or moves her body. We may think that a person who slouches is either lazy, tired, or depressed; that a person who walks with quick steps and swinging arms to match is tense, nervous, or at least in a hurry; that a person who slumps in a chair with head cocked to one side resting on a hand is bored or tired. Whether or not we are correct in these assumptions is in one sense unimportant; the fact remains that we constantly assign meaning to the body positions and movements of others.

There have been various methods devised to study bodily aspects of nonverbal communication. One of these was developed by Albert Scheflin, who has studied the body movements and positions of people involved in interaction with one another. Scheflin has found that within an interpersonal setting the body movements of the people involved can be divided into units which correspond to the verbal portion of the messages being exchanged and, therefore, recur systematically over time. The three kinds of units which Scheflin has identified are the *point,* the *position,* and the *presentation.*[2] The point, which, as Scheflin says, roughly corresponds to "making a point" in a conversation, occurrs after every few sentences which a person speaks. At the end of a few sentences, the speaker may make very slight body movements, such as changing the position of the head, which indicate the conclusion of one point. The second unit, the position, is indicated by a much greater movement of the body, such as leaning forward or backward from the waist. Scheflin explains that positions last longer than points and correspond verbally "to a point of view that an interactant may take in an interaction." He gives the following example of a change in position:

> Imagine a participant in a conference leaning back in his chair, smoking, remaining silent as another person expresses a point of view. The listener experiences growing disagreement and decides finally that he must state his viewpoint. His shift begins. He tamps out his cigarette, uncrosses his

> legs, leans forward, and, perhaps with some gesture, begins his exposition.[3]

The last unit of body movement which Scheflin has studied is the presentation. It "consists of the totality of one person's positions in a given interaction." Presentations may be marked by a person changing his place in the room or by completely leaving the setting.

It is important to note that these units of movement do not occur in isolation but rather within the context of the interaction. For example, the units may be used to signal when one person expects a response from another, or perhaps to change the course of an interaction, as when a person leaves the room. Scheflin calls these units of movement *markers* because in some way they mark or signal some kind of change in the ongoing interaction. He explains that each of us exhibits a limited number of these markers but that we use them over and over again within the context of any single interaction. In so doing, Scheflin explains, our nonverbal behavior becomes "patterned and systematic."

Scheflin has termed one pattern occurring repeatedly within an interpersonal setting *quasi-courtship behavior.*[4] He explains that quasi-coutrship behavior is similar to traditional courtship behavior except that it includes qualifiers which indicate that sexual consummation is not to be expected. According to Scheflin, quasi-courtship behavior can include such things as tensing the facial and bodily muscles, which makes a person appear brighter and more alert, and preening behavior like stroking the hair or clothing. Quasi-courtship behavior also can include the positioning of the body in relation to another or others in the setting. Look at the series of pictures in figure 10. Can you identify which elements of behavior Scheflin would term quasi-courtship?

Remember again that we are not interested in these patterns of behavior for themselves but rather for their message value and its effect on the ongoing interaction

Figure 10. *Quasi–Courtship Behavior*
(a) Important elements here might be the tilted position of the young woman's body and head, her slightly parted lips, her shining eyes. Would you assign meaning to any of these elements?

(b) This picture illustrates a blatant example of preening behavior. Would you assign any meaning to this young woman's hair patting?

Figure 10. *Quasi-courtship Behavior*
(c) With both hands in his pockets, this young man appears to have his pelvis thrust forward. Would you assign any meaning to this position?

(d) This young woman has high muscle tonus in her face and bright, shining eyes. She has oriented her body in the direction of the person to whom she is speaking. Would you assign any meaning to these elements?

between people. Along these lines one of the most obvious kinds of nonverbal communication behavior between people is touching. In the chapter on the senses, we discussed how in our society touching another person is rather strictly regulated. In a study performed with students, Sidney Jourard in 1966 found that various parts of the body were quite often touched while others were very infrequently touched. Look at Figure 11. Do Jourard's findings match your own experiences?

Another area of bodily nonverbal communication behavior which has been studied a great deal is that of arm and hand gestures. Think of the ways in which we use our arms and hands to communicate with others! In many instances, we can use them to replace all verbal communication—for example, beckoning with an index finger or hand indicating "come here," or placing an index finger against a thumb indicating "O.K.," or raising a middle finger saying, to put it nicely, "up yours." We also use arms and hands to illustrate what we are saying. For example, if I say "My new sheep dog is about this long and this high," I really need more than words to give meaning to my message. For another example, try saying the phrase "Just let me say . . . " while making the illustrated hand movements shown in figure 12. Gestures also can be used as emphasis; you punctuate "I won't go!" by slamming a clenched fist into the other hand.

To a large degree, gestures are culturally learned, and the same movements may have very different meanings in different societies. Try various movements of your hands, arms, and body, and decide what meaning you would give to the movement. For example, try putting your hand over your heart and leaning forward . . . now lean backward. What meanings would you give to these movements? Or put your hand to your forehead with the palm turned in, then turn it out. Would you say these two movements had different meanings? Watch your own and other people's

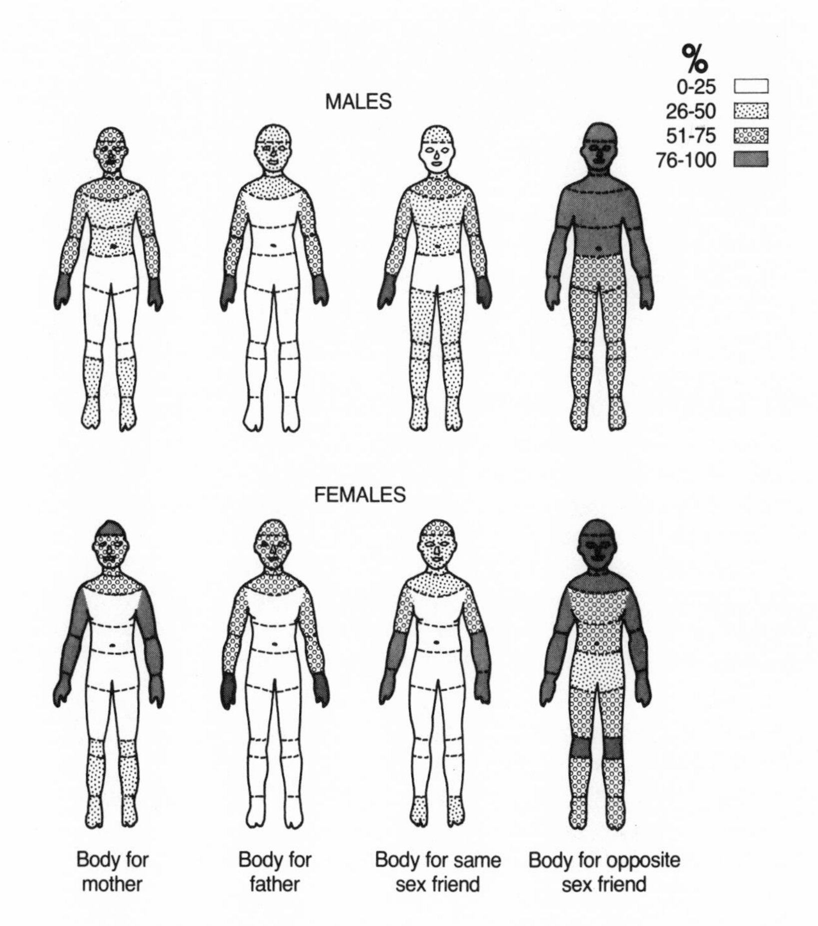

Figure 11. *Body for Others*
This diagram shows what percentage of students out of a total of 168 males and 140 females reported being touched on various areas of their bodies by the people indicated along the bottom of the diagram. For example, 76-100% of the male students reported being touched by their "opposite sex friend" on all areas of the body above the waist.

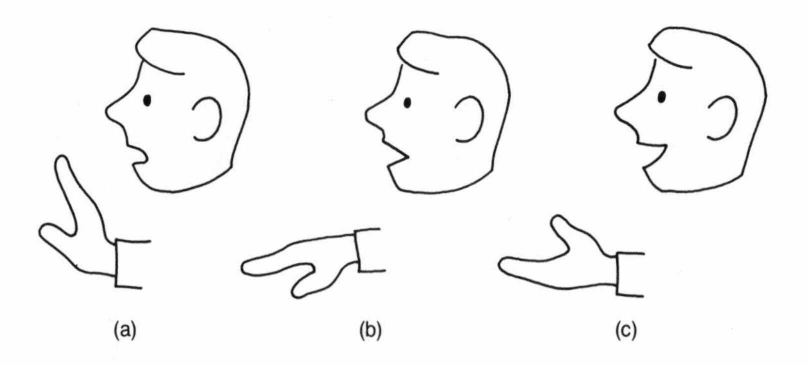

Figure 12. *Illustrating*
With the hand held up (a) the message is likely to be: "Wait, let me say . . ." With the palm down (b), the message is more likely to imply: "Now let me tell you how it really is. . . ." With the palm up (c), the underlying message may be: "Well, just let me say I think that . . ." Or: "It seems to me . . ."

gestures and see if you can discover what meanings the various movements have for you.

Facial Expressions

The final area of bodily nonverbal communication behavior is that of facial expressions. Look at the pictures in figure 13. What would you say about the people in each picture?

In many ways we use facial expressions in the same ways we use body gestures. From studies, however, it has been found that when looking at still photographs of people's faces, judges are more likely to agree on what affect state is being expressed than when they observe pictures of the body.[5] This may be because we have become better at receiving cues from a person's face since that is where we usually look when interacting with another. It also may be that the face often is more expressive than the body and changes more rapidly and more frequently.

Look at yourself in a mirror. Try moving your mouth, eyes, and cheek muscles in all different ways. What would you say about each expression you see reflected back to you?

PARALINGUISTICS

At the beginning of this chapter, we said that any message may be composed of two parts: the verbal and the nonverbal. There is, however, one area of nonverbal communication which falls between the verbal and the nonverbal. It has to do with *how* the words of the verbal portion of the message are said. It is nonverbal in that it does not deal with the language used per se but rather with the volume, tone, rate, pitch, inflection, and so forth that the speaker uses. For example, say the following sentence with emphasis on the word italicized:

Do you want me to go?
Do *you* want me to go?
Do you *want* me to go?
Do you want *me* to go?
Do you want me to *go?*

As you can see, if someone were to send this message to you, the meaning you assigned to it would depend upon the emphasis the other person used. This area of nonverbal communication is known as *paralinguistics* since it is above, beyond, or in addition to the specific language used. This form of nonverbal communication allows a speaker to indicate to another *how the message is to be take*n and for this reason many people have great difficulty in writing letters since they have to try and convey their meaning through the verbal portion of the message alone.

Most of us are very much attuned to the paralinguistic aspects of messages. From these and other nonverbal cues we try to decide if someone is being honest in

Figure 13. *Facial Expressions*
Specifically what about each expression is important to you in assigning meaning to it?

I do my thing
and you do your thing.
I am not in this world
to live up to your
expectations
And you are not in this
world to live up to mine.
You are you and I am I.
And if by chance we find
each other,
It's beautiful.

what he or she is saying and, therefore, whether or not we can trust that person. For example, when someone says to you "But I love you!" how do you "know" whether or not she or he means it?

Uses of Nonverbal Communication

The area of nonverbal communication is large, and we have indicated only some of the ways it has been studied. From what we have discussed, however, you can see that the nonverbal aspects of a message are important and that they are related to the verbal portions in many ways. In discussing this relationship, Mark Knapp has identified six ways the nonverbal aspects may relate to the verbal. These are as follows:

1. **repeating**—A nonverbal cue can repeat what was said verbally, as when someone says "He ran toward Main Street" and points in that direction.
2. **contradicting**—A nonverbal cue can contradict what was said verbally, as when someone says "I'm not angry" in a loud voice with face flushed and hands clenched. As Knapp points out, in case of contradictory cues, we are much more likely to trust the nonverbal aspects.
3. **substituting**—A nonverbal cue can substitute for a verbal cue, as when someone says something to you which you do not believe and with head down you peer at them with raised eyebrows all of which clearly says "Ah, come on!"
4. **complementing**—A nonverbal cue can complement, elaborate, or modify a verbal cue, as when someone says "I love you!" with bright eyes and a big smile on his face.
5. **accenting**—A nonverbal cue can accent a certain part of a verbal message, as when someone says "I don't want you to do that again!" and slams a hand on the table when saying the word "don't."
6. **relating and regulating**—A nonverbal cue can regulate the flow of verbal communication, as when someone raises his hand indicating he wants to speak.[6]

TRANSACTIONAL MODEL OF COMMUNICATION

At the close of the previous chapter on language, we stressed that the meaning for words is not contained in the words themselves but is in or is evolved by the people in an interaction. The same thing can be said for the nonverbal cues available in a given situation. These cues are available from the environment (perhaps $\mathbf{C_{PU}}$ or $\mathbf{C_{PR}}$) as illustrated in the discussion on the uses of space or from such

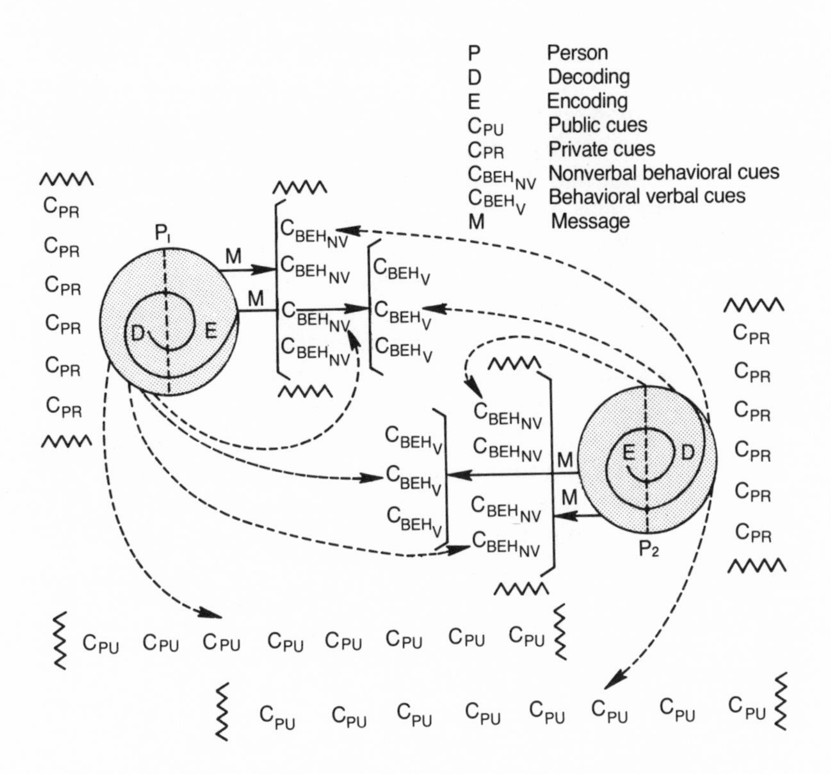

Figure 14. *The Transactional Model of Communication*

things as the dress, movements, and expressions of all the people involved in the situation ($C_{BEH_{NV}}$).

When referring to Barnlund's model, it is important that although we simultaneously encode and decode verbal and nonverbal messages, we *may* be more aware of the process with verbal communication than with nonverbal. If one person says something to another, she is aware that she is speaking. She also may be aware of some of her nonverbal cues to which they both assign meaning. It is more likely, however, that the other person can assign meaning to the nonverbal than to the verbal cues of which the speaker is unaware.

We can think of this difference as being between "what" and "that." Using the same example, if someone says something to another, she may not know "what" the thing she has said means to him, but she will know "that" she said something. If on the other hand, while she is speaking, she makes a gesture of which she is unaware, not only will she not know "what" it means to the other person, she will not even know "that" she did it.

This same process operates in a slightly different way for the other person involved in the interaction. For example, he will be aware that she has said something, and he will process the cue to decide what it means to him. He may be very unaware, however, that he also is assigning meaning to one of her gestures. And this is one of the reasons we must be even more alert to our perception of nonverbal communication than to verbal. It also is another example of Barnlund's final communication postulate: "Communication is complex."

NOTES

1. Edward T. Hall, *The Hidden Dimension* (Garden City, N.Y.: Doubleday and Co., 1966), pp. 95–105.

2. Albert E. Scheflen, "The Significance of Posture in Communication Systems," *Psychiatry* 27 (1964): 316–31.
3. Ibid., p. 323.
4. Albert E. Scheflen, "Quasi-Courtship Behavior in Psychotherapy," *Psychiatry* 28 (1965): 245–57.
5. For example, see Paul Ekman and Wallace V. Friesen, "Head and Body Cues in the Judgment of Emotion: A Reformulation," *Perceptual and Motor Skills* 24 (1967): 711–24.
6. Mark L. Knapp, *Nonverbal Communication in Human Interacaction* (New York: Holt, Rinehart and Winston, 1972), pp. 9–12. Reprinted by permission of the publisher.

6 SELF-CONCEPT AND COMMUNICATION

In previous chapters we have discussed the sense organs and the processes of perception which facilitate both verbal and nonverbal communication. Throughout these discuss-ions it may have seemed that while everything which was said is true, it all does not quite present human beings as unique individuals. Each of us has a body which functions in certain ways and a mind which allows us to classify and communicate with the world around us, but most of us feel that there is something more—something unique—which, even if many of the other trappings were taken away, would still remain. Theoretically, we can talk about these feelings as being a part of the self, self-concept, or self-image.

Generally, a self-concept can be thought of as being all the feelings a person has about himself or herself. It is important to realize that this "picture" we have of ourselves is *learned* over many years and that although some aspects

Figure 1. *Is One of These "Me's" the REAL One?*

may remain constant over time, our self-images can change drastically from situation to situation. In fact, in one way it is difficult to distinguish between "self-concept" and "situation" since each of these influences the other. How we see ourselves at any given time depends greatly upon the situation we are in, and how we approach a situation and the people in it is largely determined by how we see ourselves.

Suppose, for example, you go to a party at which you know few people. If you see yourself as a lively, outgoing, fun-loving person, you will probably go to the party reasonably self-assured, expecting to meet and talk with many new people. In other words, how you see yourself will determine how you expect to behave in this situation. Imagine that you arrive at the party and approach the situation exactly as you had expected. You begin to meet and talk with a few people and generally enjoy yourself. After a little while, however, you realize that most of the people there are somewhat older than you, more sophisticated, more boistrous, and so forth. In fact, as the evening progresses, you get the feeling that the party is definitely getting out of hand even though everyone else seems to be having a grand time! You may find yourself sitting quietly in a chair, slowly sipping your drink, and wondering why you cannot seem to get into the swing of things. Perhaps you decide after all that you are a bit shy and not nearly so outgoing as you had thought. Although these may not be long-lasting feelings, they will influence how you behave for the moment and perhaps how you approach similar situations in the future.

This example illustrates that although we feel our self-concept is a private and internal feeling, it is, in fact, based largely upon our interactions with others over time. In other words, a person's *self-concept is developed, maintained, and changed through some form of interpersonal communication.*[1] If you doubt this, try to decide where, if not from others, you got certain feelings you have about yourself. And since, as we said before, the influence of self and situation works in both directions, you may be able to discover ways in which your self-image has influenced situations you have been in and other people involved in those situations.

So far we have been talking about the self or self-concept as if it were a "thing"—something which influences and is influenced. This approach may be misleading since the self obviously is not something that is located somewhere inside one's body like a liver or a brain. Although that may sound ridiculous, many people do tend to feel that their "real self" is located somewhere inside their head or between their ribs very close to the heart. For centuries philosphers have argued about the answer to the question "What is the self?" That question, very similiar to the one about the number of angels which can comfortably dance on the head of a pin, has no concrete answer but may be worth pondering.

For now, however, we can deal strictly with the self-concept or how each of us sees himself or herself. Look again at that sentence. Simply the way it is worded implies that each of us has *a* self-concept, in other words, that we each see ourselves in *a* certain way. From the example of the party, it is apparent that this is not true. And here we get into the problem of how to talk about the idea of "self-concept."

Like many other psychological terms, self-concept is a *hypothetical construct.* It is a concept which researchers have developed in order to study the internal states of an organism and how these states affect and are affected by the external environment. Think about the hypothetical construct *intelligence.* As we all know, intelligence is not a physical reality—it cannot be seen, felt, or weighed. By assuming that such a construct exists, however, we can study the effects of external stimuli, for example, education, upon the internal states of an individual, in this case, the development of intelligence, or, conversely, the effects of the internal state (level of intelligence) upon external factors (achievement in school). Put more simply, many researchers have studied the effects of education upon the level of one's intelligence while others have examined the influence of level of intelligence on scholastic success or failure.

We can see that in this way a hypothetical construct is not so much a *structure* as a *process* which gets us back to the earlier statement that the self-concept cannot be thought of as a structure or a thing. Rather, self-concept should be regarded as an internal *process* whose elements are all those thoughts and feelings about oneself that one has learned through contact with others in the environment.

In exactly the same way that intelligence has been studied, we can talk about the self-concept as being an internal state of the individual at any given moment. We can then attempt to isolate the external stimuli which affect this internal state and suggest ways in which this internal state may affect external factors. In both cases the "affect" is achieved or observed through interpersonal communication situations. Let us look at some ways in which the self-concept may be affected by external stimuli.

DEVELOPMENT OF SELF-CONCEPT

You have probably heard the old comedy line "I started this life as a very small child." Most of us, therefore, have had a similiar beginning. As very small children we were, more than at any other time in our life, totally accepted for what we were and for what we did. Since we could not be expected to know much about what we were supposed to do, most of what we did was all right. These beautiful months, however, did not last very long. Since part of the responsibilities of being a parent is to help a child learn to become a functioning member of the society, our parents, or parental figures, trained us in many ways and quickly we learned that everything we did and wanted to do was not all right with them. We learned that the bathroom was not just another room in the house but one where we were expected to go whenever necessary. . . preferably before it was too late. We learned there were certain ways of eating which were more acceptable than others and certain ways of treating our brothers and sisters which were preferable at least to them and to our parents. We learned there were certain parts of our bodies which we should not display in public. We learned there were specific names for things around us and that if we used the right one, we more often got what we wanted. In general, we learned that some things we did brought approval and praise from our parents and that other things brought disapproval and possibly punishment. When we did things that pleased our parents, we felt loved—we were "good." But when we incurred their displeasure, we felt unloved—"bad."

Harry Stack Sullivan explains this process as the development of what he calls the *good me* and the *bad me.*[2] Since behavior associated with the "bad me" can cause one to feel unloved and anxious, much of this behavior is eliminated or suppressed so that children may receive the warmth and approval and consequently the nonanxious feeling they like. In general we can see, then, that as small children our overt behavior was largely shaped by those around us and for most of us the most important people around us at this time were our parents.

As one grows older, other people begin to take on increasing importance. Acceptance by playmates, teachers, and friends of both sexes becomes very important. In many ways, however, a person simply adds these later influences to what he has already learned about himself, and many people may go through life holding onto their original general categories of *good me* and *bad me* even though with increasing maturity these categories are no longer sufficient or workable.

In our discussion of perception and language, we said that our perceptions of the world depend largely upon the categories and labels we have learned. As human beings we have the ability not only to be conscious as do other animals but also to be self-conscious. In other words, one of the "objects" in our world which we perceive is ourselves, and our perception of self works the same as does our perception of anything else. Once we have learned to categorize our behavior and what labels to apply to those categories, it is very difficult to alter these perceptions, our views of and feelings toward ourselves. Later we will discuss how we may be able to become aware of how we see ourselves and to alter these perceptions if necessary, but for now let us look at how our development of self-concept continues after the original beginnings of our self-perceptions.

William James, one of the earliest psychological theorists who focused on the self, defined the self as being composed of the *I*, which he termed the *Knower,* and the *me,* or that which is *Known.*[3] He explained that the me, or the things we can know about ourselves, is composed of three aspects: (1) the *material me,* including our homes, our families, and our possessions; (2) the *social me*, consisting of the recognition we get from others or groups of others; (3) the *spiritual me*, defined as all of our states of consciousness, emotions, and desires. He explained further that the feeling we have for ourselves, often called our *self-esteem*, is determined by those things which we are successful at doing as compared with those things which we would like to do, or as he put it:

$$\text{self-esteem} = \frac{\text{success}}{\text{pretensions}}$$

From this formula we can see that according to James, a person can increase his level of self-esteem by either increasing the numerator, success, or decreasing the denominator, pretensions. For example, being good in athletics is very important to many young men. Let us sppose that one young basketball player is feeling bad about himself because he has not scored an average of 30 points a game as he feels he should. According to James' formula, he can either spend all his spare time practicing until he achieves this goal or he can decide that scoring an average of 30 points is just unrealistic for him and set his goal at 15–20 points a game. In either case, since being good in athletics is important to him, when he achieves his goal, his level of self-esteem will rise.

Charles Horton Cooley, writing a few years after James, suggested that the most important aspect of the self was what James had called the *social me.* Cooley's phrase *looking glass self* meant that we see ourselves reflected in the eyes of others and take on their attitudes toward us as our own.[4]

Combining the theories of James and Cooley, we see that how we feel about ourselves is largely determined by how others feel about us. Furthermore, those things by which we judge ourselves—our goals and our successes—are largely determined by the groups of people with whom we are in contact. In writing about group influence of this type, social psychologists have found it helpful to differentiate between two types of groups. First there is what has become known as a *membership group.* This type of group would be one to which you actually belong such as your family, your ethnic group, your work group, your friendship groups. From these groups we learn certain standards which we may feel we should meet. Suppose in a person's family, education and learning are very important. If so, it is probably important to the individual to do well in school or, more generally, to appear to be smart. It probably would be quite surprising to such an individual to meet someone for whom "appearing to be smart" had very little importance.

The second type of group which may affect how we see and feel about ourselves has been called a *reference group.* A reference group differs from a membership group in that we do not actually belong to such a group but we do have a desire to belong or at least to be like the members of the group. For example, many of us are influenced by such groups when we are preparing ourselves for a specific profession. Although we are not yet part of a particular professional group, we may begin to use that group's standards in evaluating ourselves. Such influence obviously is not restricted to professional groups but may operate in relation to others such as social and religious groups. In all cases, however, if how we see and feel about ourselves is affected by our perceptions of the standards of a group to which we would like to belong, then it is being influenced by one or more reference groups.

To explain the effect of group influence on an individual, Leon Festinger originally developed the idea of *social comparison processes.*[5] It was Festinger's theory that as human beings we have an intrinsic desire to evaluate our opinions and abilities, and that when there is an objective, nonsocial method of making these evaluations, we will use it. When there is no way to judge objectively our own opinions or abilities, however, we will use those of others as standards. Actually, because there *is* no purely objective way to evaluate most of our opinions, we are almost entirely dependent upon others to let us know how "good" or how "bad" any one of our opinions is. To some extent, the same thing is true for our abilities. A logical response to a question such as "How good are you at ____?" is, "In comparison to what?" For example, how good are you at tennis or swimming or getting good grades? You may not be very good at tennis compared with Billie Jean King, or at swimming compared with Mark Spitz, or at getting good grades compared with the valedictorian. But how good are you at tennis compared with some of your friends? Or how good a swimmer are you compared with a younger brother or sister?

Following the theories of group influence and of social comparison processes, it appears that how we learn to see and evaluate ourselves depends largely upon the groups around us with whom we compare ourselves. Although later in life we choose for ourselves the groups we wish to join, as small children these groups were chosen for us for the most part and therefore, our concept of self tended to develop under influences selected for us by someone else.

MAINTAINING THE SELF-CONCEPT

As we have said, it is much more helpful to think of self-concept as a *process,* rather than a structure. In the first chapter we explained that a process by its very nature is dynamic rather than static. Therefore, it is inaccurate to say that at some point our self-concept is formed and remains with us throughout life. As we have seen, however, we learn very early how to classify and label our world, and these original categories are very difficult to change. In relation to ourselves we learn that certain behaviors are good and certain behaviors are bad. In general, little boys learn that it is good to be rough and tough and bad to be sensitive and helpless, and little girls learn the opposite. As we grow older we may retain these original categories—seeing and evaluating ourselves along the lines we learned as children. If a young woman sees herself as sensitive and somewhat helpless, she may have relatively good feelings towards herself. If, however, she does something which she would classify as "aggressive", she may feel bad about herself—she is not being the kind of person she is "supposed" to be. Or, more likely, she will say to herself that she was just not being "herself" at that particular moment.

That last sentence is important, because it suggests that we have a need to *maintain* our view of ourselves. We expect things to be as we "know" them to be; in other words, we expect things to be consistent with our ideas of them. Since we are part of the world we perceive, think how much more difficult it would be to recategorize and reevaluate ourselves!

Our need to maintain the images and feelings we have for ourselves is often closely related to our choice of groups to relate to. Many of us choose groups that will lend support to our existing views of ourselves; the similarity between their standards and our own helps us to feel comfortable and very much "ourselves."

We may think of this process as being one of *self-confirmation.* Since we use others to evaluate ourselves, we tend to select associates who will confirm the views we have of ourselves. When we communicate with others, we may tend to see or to perceive only those expressions and reactions which coincide with our views of ourselves. And if some behavior toward us on the part of another person does not fit with how we see ourselves, we tend to say that *the other person* was not acting like himself at that moment rather than to reevaluate a particular perception of our own.

Our desire to see ourselves in a certain way affects not only what kinds of information we can take in from others but also the kinds of things others are permitted to know about us. We can look at this process from many different points of view. Think about a group of friends you are often with. You probably chose this group partly because you agree on many things, partly because the members see you the way you see yourself, or perhaps because of the way you like to see yourself. For whatever the reason or reasons, you originally chose to be part of the group, by now your friends probably expect you to act in a certain way. This "certain way" includes not only behavior which is in line with the standards of the group, for example, preferring a "free" lifestyle, but also behavior which is specifically yours. Perhaps you are thought of as "always happy" or "always joking" or "always glum." In order for you to continue to feel confirmed by this group, it may be necessary for you to hide the fact that you are sometimes sad, or sometimes serious or sometimes happy. And although hiding these feelings from others may not change completely the way you see yourself, it is difficult to feel totally accepted by, or confirmed by, other people when compelled to hide important aspects of yourself from them.

Our desire to see ourselves and to have other people see us in a certain way can thus hinder open communication with others and perhaps even with ourselves. Trying to maintain a consistent image or role by adhering to a set of specific prescribed behaviors can result in the same kind of alienation. Imagine that you want to become a teacher. Even though not yet a member of that group, you may begin to use the standards of that group to evaluate yourself. You thereby begin to copy some of the behavior you see as befitting the "teacher role"—behavior which may or may not be alien to you. Throughout our lives we are required to learn how to "perform" many different roles. We are expected to be children, students, mothers, fathers, lovers, doctors, sisters, teachers, lawyers, cab drivers. . . . *How a person chooses to play a role is largely determined by how he or she sees himself or herself.*

So far we have talked about how we begin to develop images of and feelings for ourselves. We also have seen how, although our concept of ourself changes throughout our life, we attempt to maintain an image consistent with what we consider ourselves to be. We have seen that both the development and the maintenance of our self-concept is influenced by our interpersonal communication and that how we see ourselves influences how we communicate with others. A more complete understanding of one's own self-concept, and the possibility of *changing* certain aspects which are no longer helpful also are facilitated through communication with others. Let us look at some of these processes.

EXPANDING AND CHANGING THE SELF-CONCEPT

All of us play many different roles. In other words, we are expected, and expect ourselves, to behave in different ways. Each of us also has many different and often conflicting feelings. Sometimes we feel happy, sometimes sad, sometimes loving, sometimes hateful, kind and cruel, giving and selfish, gorgeous and ugly, outgoing and shy. And all of these feelings we experience are a part of us. There is no consistency to the feelings we have or to the behaviors we engage in. Does it not seem absurd, then, for us to attempt to hold on to any *one* image of ourselves, to expect that everything we do should be consistent with how we see ourselves and, even more, to expect what others say and do to us to coincide with our concept of ourselves?

In our society it seems to be a "good" thing to be consistent and a "bad" thing to be inconsistent. We have many sayings which deride those who act in incongruous ways. For example, you have heard and used the term *two-faced,* or accused another of not being "herself." The first step in getting to know oneself better may be simply to accept the fact that one does have many different feelings, and does engage in many different behaviors. In many cases these feelings and behaviors may be inconsistent with one another and/or with one's self-image. But rather than focusing on *how you see yourself, try looking at how you go about the seeing.* What kinds of categories do you have for yourself? Where did you get these categories? Are they still meaningful and important to you? For example, if you originally learned such labels as *good* and *bad,* is that still an important distinction to you? Does it make any sense to you now?

Discovering one's own classification and labeling system is an extremely difficult process. In trying to learn more about how we see ourselves, making any changes in our images which might be helpful, several theorists have suggested that the process can be facilitated through communication with others. Sidney Jourard has gone so far as to say, ". . . *no man can come to know himself except as an outcome of disclosing himself to another person.*"[6] Understandably, this may seem to be an extreme position to take. Think back, however, to our discussion on the development of self-concept. When a person just begins learning about himself, he is in no position to select information that is accurate and reject what is not. Whatever his parents originally told him about himself he had not only to accept but in many ways try to incorporate into his behavior. He was, after all, totally dependent upon them for everything he needed. They were, however, simply two people telling him *their* opinions of things and in this case their opinions about him. Although we do not necessarily hold on to all the ideas we are taught originally, the first "ways of seeing" which we learn are very important. By disclosing to a trusted friend one's basic feelings toward oneself, a person can at least begin to examine how he classifies and evaluates himself. The idea of being completely open with others is very scary for many people. This is not surprising since, as we discussed earlier, from very early in our lives we are in a sense rewarded for hiding some aspects of ourselves. Remember, however, that we said it might be helpful to disclose *fully* to at least one other *trusted* person. To be completely open with everyone certainly creates as many problems as being open with no one. It may be that in a society as complex as ours, it is better to select carefully those with whom we will work at developing an open relationship.

When we speak of self-disclosure within the context of an *open* relationship, it is obvious that the disclosure is reciprocal. In other words both, or all, people are sharing information about themselves. In order to explain this process, Joseph Luft and Harry Ingram developed a model which they referred to as the Johari Window. The window is shown in figure 2.

Think of the window as representing the personality of an individual. Quadrant 1, the open area, represents all of a person's thoughts, feelings, and behaviors which are known both to her and to another person or persons. The larger this quadrant in any particular relationship, the freer the communication.

In quadrant 2, the blind area, is all the information about one's feelings and behaviors unknown to oneself but known to others—for example, those times when we are not aware that something someone has done has made us very angry but others can easily see that we are annoyed. This area is sometimes referred to as the "bad breath" area!

Quadrant 3 is called the hidden area because informa-

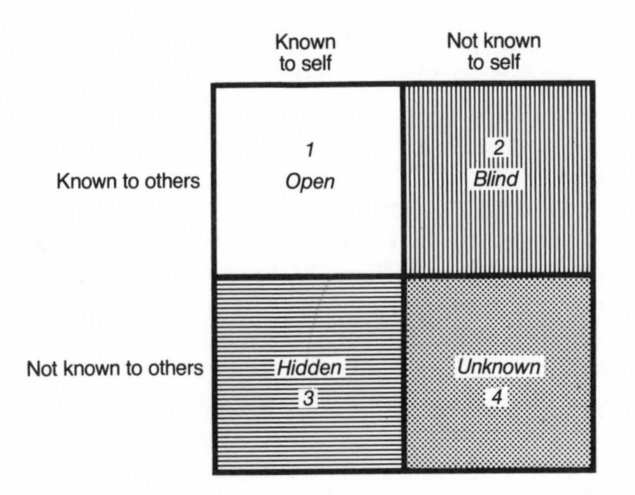

Figure 2. *The Johari Window*

tion in this quadrant is known to oneself but hidden from others. Using the same example as above, there may be many times when we are quite angry with someone and are aware of our anger but do not let the other know about it.

Quadrant 4 is called the unknown area and takes into account all those feelings and motivations which are unknown to both ourselves and to others. Often we refer to this area as the subconscious.

We do not have one Johari Window but rather we have many—perhaps there are as many as the number of people with whom we relate. And depending upon the degree of openness within any one relationship, the appearance of the window will vary. For example, perhaps the window representing your relationship with your closest friend would look something like figure 3, whereas your window in another, more casual relationship would look like figure 4.

It is important to note that moving information from one quadrant to another changes the size of both quadrants.

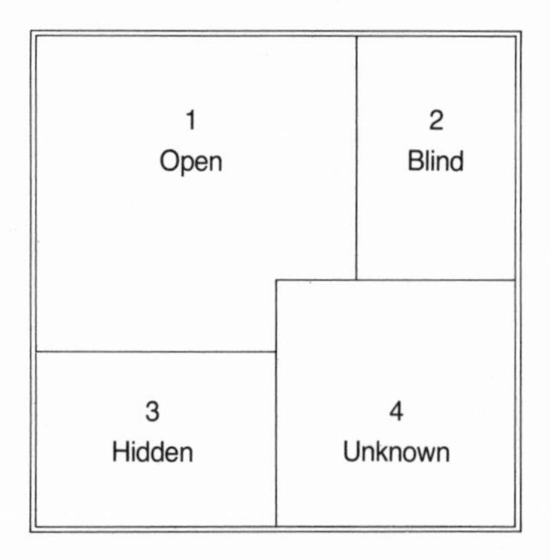

Figure 3. *An Open Window*

For example, even in the relationship with your closest friend, there may be some information which you keep hidden and some information of which you are not aware. If you suddenly disclose some information to your friend or he explains his perceptions to you, the size of the hidden or blind area will decrease slightly as the size of the open area increases, making, of course, freer communication between you.

Let us look more closely at the Johari Window for a moment. When we speak of disclosing the self to another we are not talking simply about giving the other person *information* about one's self. A person can say all sorts of things about herself such as her name, her age, where she's gone to school, things she likes and dislikes, and so forth. And another person will know her a bit better than he did before. That kind of information, however, has very little to do with her *at the moment* she is interacting with him. He would have a much greater sense of her as a person if she were to tell him more about herself right then, for example, what she's thinking about and how she's feeling in the situation and in reaction to him. This kind of information is much more helpful to each of them for several reasons. In telling

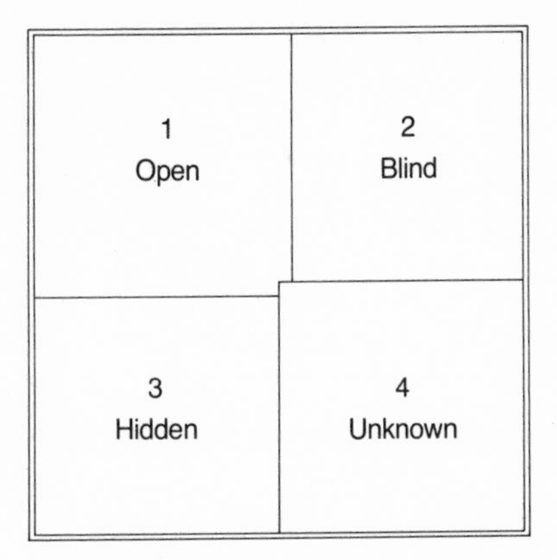

Figure 4. *A Restricted Window*

him about her feelings at the moment, she is saying something about herself and how she reacts to things, and she is also saying something about him since he is one of the things to which she is reacting. In other words, she is moving some information in her Johari Window from the hidden to the open quadrant and perhaps she is moving some information in his window from the blind to the open area.

Let us take this idea one step further. In the chapter on perception, we explained that according to Gestalt theory our perceptual processes are based upon the alteration between figure and ground, or what at any given moment stands out in importance and what recedes into the background. Speaking figuratively, it may be that at most times the individual herself is her most important figure. If this is so, then any information she gives to another about how she sees him may be saying much more about her than about him and any information he gives to her about himself, she may interpret primarily in relation to herself. In either case she may be able to move some information from either her blind or unknown area into the open quadrant, thereby knowing herself and letting the other know her, and perhaps himself, more fully.

In many of his writing, Carl Rogers refers to this type of open and honest communication between two or more people as a facilitative or helping relationship.[7] By these terms he means that each person within the relationship is helping the other person to become all he or she can be —attempting to facilitate the growth of the other. Within the context of our present discussion, this kind of growth would mean helping another person to become more "real" by learning to see himself more clearly, accepting those attributes having current relevance, and rejecting those no longer meaningful. Obviously this kind of communication can occur only within the context of a relationship where there is a great deal of trust between or among the people involved. If I am to listen to you and utilize the information you are giving me about myself, I must trust you. Even if I may not agree with everything you say or if some of what you say hurts me or frightens me, I must believe that you are being honest with me and that your goal is to help me learn more about myself and become all that I can be.

As we all know, this process is not an easy one. And, to make things even more difficult, it is probably true that before a person can come to trust another, he must have developed at least a certain degree of trust in himself. How, if not through communication with another, does a person develop this degree of self-awareness and trust?

Let us look again at Barnlund's Transactional Model of Communication. The circle represents a person in his world. As indicated in the model, the number of cues available to him from each of the sources is inestimable. In chapter 2 we discussed our sense organs as receptors of the many cues available to us. It is important to remember that as human beings we do have the capacity for great cognitive development, but we are, basically, *physical beings*—organisms—and to deny physical aspects of ourselves is to deny a very large part of us indeed.

In order to trust oneself more completely, it is perhaps

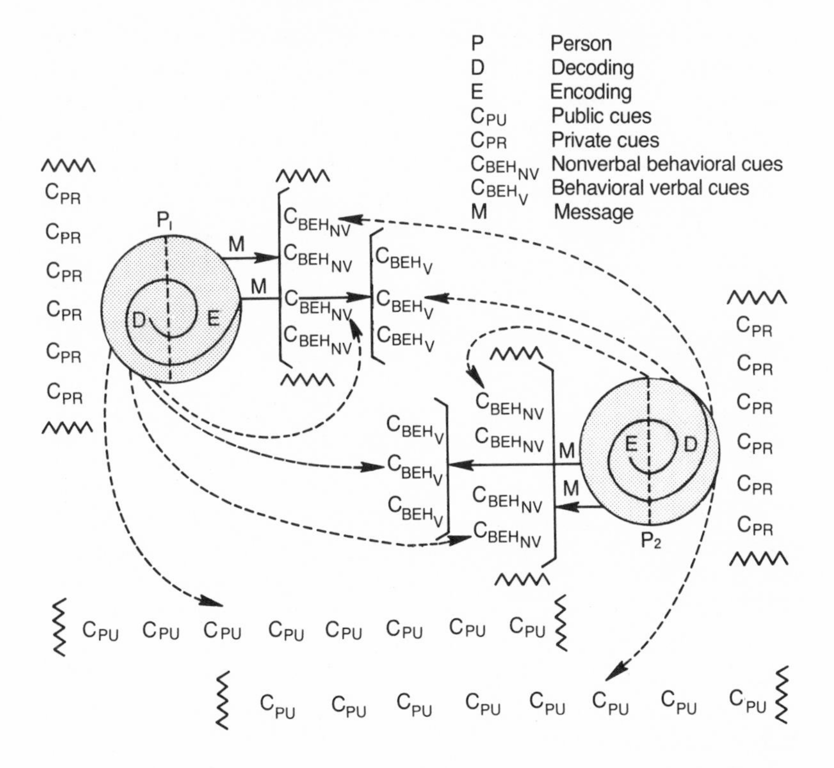

Figure 5. *The Transactional Model of Communication*

necessary for one to pay more attention to oneself as a physical being and to be in contact with as much of the world around one as possible. Rather than trying immediately to categorize and evaluate the cues available to us, a *process which we orginally learned from others,* how does what we see, smell, hear, taste, and touch make us *feel?* Rather than trying to figure out what someone "means" by what she or he is saying or what the motives are for saying it, how does the remark make us *feel?* In other words, can we develop more completely the capacity within ourselves to determine what is good for us and what is bad for us; what is pleasurable and what is unpleasurable? Can we trust ourselves to act in a way that is congruent with how we are feeling or inherently reacting to our world? And if we can to some extent develop this degree of trust within ourselves, then we can more accurately decide whether or not it is reasonable to trust another person with whom we relate.

NOTES

1. The general outline for this discussion was adapted from "Some Interpersonal Aspects of Self-Conformation," in *Inter-terpersonal Dynamics*, ed. Warren Bennis et al. (Homewood, Ill.: The Dorsey Press, 1968), pp. 207–26.
2. Harry Stack Sullivan, *The Interpersonal Theory of Psychiatry* (New York: W. W. Norton and Co., 1953).
3. William James, *Psychology: The Briefer Course* (1892; reprint ed., New York: Harper and Row, 1961), pp. 43–83.
4. Charles Horton Cooley, *Human Nature and the Social Order* (New York: Charles Scribner's Sons, 1902).
5. Leon Festinger, "A Theory of Social Comparison Processes," *Human Relations* 7 (1954): 117–40.
6. Sidney M. Jourard, *The Transparent Self*, Rev ed. (New York: Van Nostrand Reinhold Co., 1971), p. 6.
7. For example, see Carl Rogers, *On Becoming A Person* (Boston: Houghton Mifflin Co., 1961).

7 PATTERNS OF COMMUNICATION

Think about a particular group you are part of, for example, a group of friends you see often. No matter how many people are involved, we can think of this group as comprising a *system*—a communication system—with two important aspects. First, there are components or *elements;* in other words, there are parts to the system. The elements of your group would be the people—your friends and yourself. The second important aspect of any system is the *interrelationship* of the elements. The people—the elements—are related or connected to one another by the messages they exchange, thus holding the system together by communication. Since communication is of interest here, we are more concerned with the *messages* exchanged between the people than we are in the characteristics of the people themselves.

A SYSTEMS APPROACH TO COMMUNICATION

Within the context of systems theory, a human group is an *open* as opposed to a *closed* system because it exchanges *information* with its environment. We know that you and your friends do not exist in a vacuum, as does a closed system, but rather you interact in various ways with the surrounding environment.

As an open system a human group has several properties which are important to remember when studying the communication among the people in that group. The first of these properties is *wholeness,* meaning simply that a change in any one part of the system will cause a change in the other parts of the system. This property is seen most easily when someone either enters or leaves a group; the other people in the group will react in some way to this change.

An open system, has a second property, quite similar to wholeness. Suppose that you have been in your room or apartment with three of your friends for several hours. Suddenly, a fourth friend, who also is often part of this group, arrives. We know that the addition of another person will change what has been going on in the group, as each person in the group reacts to the new person. In other words, it will not be "the same group plus one more," but in many respects, it will be a new group. In systems theory this property of a group is known as *nonsummativity;* which means that one cannot simply add together the personality characteristics of a group of people and expect to describe that group. Thus we cannot add the traits of your fourth friend to those of you and your other friends and describe the new group.

From this example we can see why when studying interpersonal communication we are not so interested in the inherent characteristics of the individuals involved as we are in studying how the people are related to one another, which is achieved and manifested through the messages they exchange.

Taking this idea one step further, we can see that if we want to understand a certain communication system, it is not enough to know about the individuals involved and the state of their relationship to one another at any given time. For example, if two people are not speaking to one another, for us to say that it is because one of them has a bad temper does not tell us *how* the system arrived at that point. Since a change in any one part of a system will affect all the other parts, a system can arrive at a certain point in many different ways.

That last sentence defines a third property of an open system—*equifinality.* If a couple is not speaking to each other, obviously we do not know why unless we have observed their communication up to this point.

In a sense, what we are saying here is similar to the discussion in the first chapter, of the circular though unrepeatable nature of communication. Remember we said that communication tends to evolve through a spiral process so that information which is based on previous information is constantly being *fed back* into the system. Only by studying the evolution of this process can we understand any specific communication system or the *relationship* between people.

In the chapters on language and on nonverbal communication we studied the various *forms* a message may take. In order to study the process of communication or the way in which a system maintains, changes, or destroys itself, however, we need to look not only at the message forms within the system but also at the *effects* of those messages upon the system.

INTERPERSONAL MESSAGES

In attempting to study the effects of messages within a communication system, Paul Watzlawick, Janet Beavin, and Don Jackson have suggested the terms *content* and *relationship* as one way of studying the effects of the messages exchanged.[1] It is their contention that any message exchanged among people contains both a *content* aspect, the informational component, and a *relationship* aspect, indicating how the message is to be taken. If one person says to another "You're stupid!!" and then with a smile and a laugh says "I was only kidding," he has very blatantly indicated how the other was supposed to take his original message. In the same way if, with a teasing and pouty tone or look, someone says "I hate you," in all probability the other person will know that he is just kidding.

Very often, although not always, the *content* aspect of a message is carried through the verbal channel and the *relationship* aspect is carried through one of the nonverbal channels. And remember that if the verbal and the nonverbal aspects of a message are consistent, everything is fine; however, if they are contradictory, we tend to pay more attention to the nonverbal aspects, as in the examples in the preceding paragraph.

There are also other times when we tend to be more concerned with the relationship aspect of a message than with the content aspect. Often when we are, for some reason, uncertain of our relationship with another, we focus considerably more on the relationship aspects of the other's messages. For example, if we are meeting someone for the first time, we may be much more concerned about trying to decide how to take her messages than we are with the information being offered. In other words, we are most concerned with deciding how this new person sees us, how she sees herself, how she sees us seeing her, and so on.

We also can become unsure of an ongoing relationship

we have with another, and when this happens, again we tend to focus on the relationship components of the messages exchanged. Pretend you have done something which greatly annoyed a very close friend. Perhaps to smooth things over, you suggest taking him to his favorite restaurant for dinner. The dialogue might be something like this:

> *You:* Let's go to Boswell's for dinner tonight . . . my treat!
> *Him:* No. I really don't feel like going there now.

From a content and relationship viewpoint, how would you analyze these two statements? My guess would be that he had focused on the relationship component of your message and had declined a reconciliation, and you were probably left feeling that his statement would have more appropriately ended with the words *with you.*

When we study a communication system, we are interested in how the system maintains and/or changes itself. In other words, we are interested in the interrelatedness of the system, which is performed by the messages exchanged within the system and specified in the *relationship* aspects of the messages.

To predict what will happen within a system or to correct a faulty system, as in intensive family therapy, researchers have various ways of looking at the *patterns* which may be observable in the relationship components of the messages exchanged among the people in the system. Let us look at some of the ways that have been developed.

Watzlawick, Beavin, and Jackson

As one way of viewing the various patterns of message exchange within a system, Watzlawick, Beavin, and Jackson have suggested the terms *complementary* and *symmetrical.*[2] They have said that "*all communicational interchanges are either symmetrical or complementary, depending on whether they are based on equality or difference.*"[3] In other words, the relationship components of the messages exchanged by two or more people within a system suggest that they see the others within the system as either equal to them or different from them. In a symmetrical interchange, all people within the system would approach one another on an equal basis. If two people were involved in an exchange in which they saw each other as equals, their interaction would be symmetrical. If, on the other hand, the relationship components of their messages indicated that one of them was different in some way, for example, one was superior and one inferior, their interaction would be complementary.

Watzlawick, Beavin, and Jackson suggest that an ongoing relationship can be seen as either more or less symmetrical or complementary. Once the system has been studied, predictions can be made about "what will happen next" based upon the symmetrical or complementary nature of the relationship aspects of the messages exchanged. There is nothing *necessarily* good or bad about either of these patterns, but as Watzlawick, Beavin, and Jackson explain, either pattern can get out of hand and develop into an unhealthy relationship. They describe, for example *escalating symmetry,* in which all the people in the system actively seek to be "more equal" than the others. Or *rigid complementarity,* where one person demands that she be regarded by another in a way that does not correspond to the way the other does see her.

In studying patterns in the relationship aspects of the messages people exchange, it is important to realize that the people involved may not only see their relationship differently from an outside observer, but actually may not agree among themselves on the existing pattern. The perception of a pattern is the same as any other perception—two people may see the "same thing" very differently.

In trying to explain why two people may not agree on how their relationship is organized or patterned, Watzlawick, Beavin, and Jackson have suggested that the difference may be based upon a disagreement over the *punctuation* of a sequence of events. They offer the following example:

Suppose a couple have a marital problem to which he contributes passive withdrawal, while her 50 percent is nagging criticism. In explaining their frustrations, the husband will state that withdrawal is his only *defense against* her nagging, while she will label this explanation a gross and willful distortion of what "really" happens in their marriage: namely, that she is critical of him *because of* his passivity. Stripped of all ephemeral and fortuitous elements, their fights consist in a monotonous exchange of the messages "I withdraw because you nag" and "I nag because you withdraw. . . . Represented graphically, with an arbitrary beginning point, their interaction looks something like figure 1:

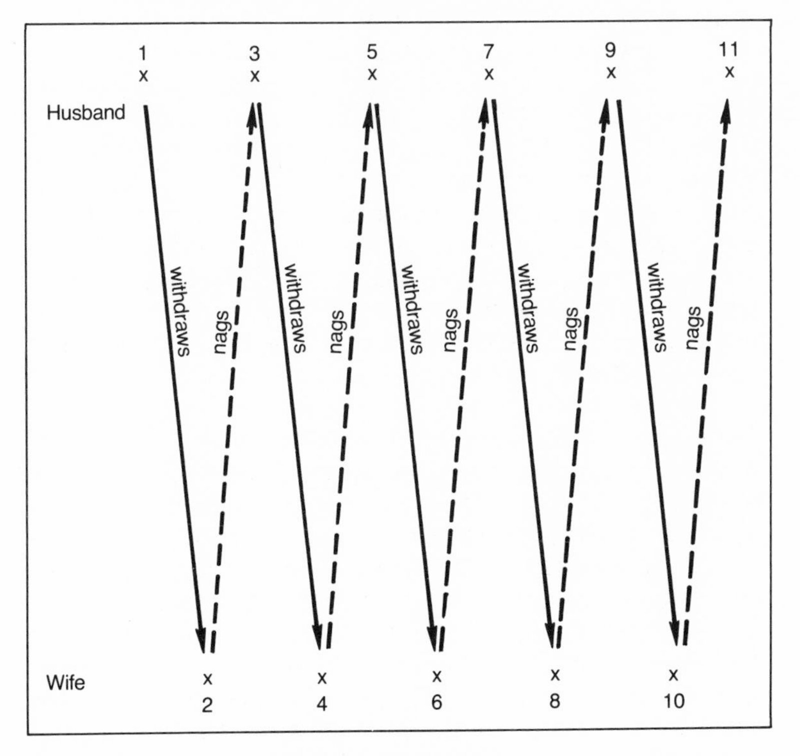

Figure 1. *Punctuation*

> It can be seen that the husband perceives only triads 2-3-4, 4-5-6, 6-7-8, etc., where his behavior (solid arrows) is "merely" a response to her behavior (the broken arrows). With her it is exactly the other way around; she punctuates the sequence of events into the triads 1-2-3, 3-4-5, 5-6-7, etc, and sees herself as only reacting to, but not determining, her busband's behavior.[4]

One way, then, of studying the interrelatedness of a communication system is to focus on the relationship aspect of the messages exchanged in an attempt to discover whether they suggest symmetry or complementarity. If by doing this a pattern can be discovered, then predictions about what will happen within the system can be made. One needs to be aware, however, of when the observation was begun so that the factor of punctuation can be taken into account.

Berne

Another way of discovering patterns within a communication system has been suggested by Eric Berne. Many of us are familiar with his theories as explained in his book *Games People Play*[5] and as popularized by Thomas Harris in *I'm O.K., You're O.K.*[6] Berne says that each of us has three ego states which are systems of feelings accompanied by related sets of behavior patterns. The three ego states are the parent, the adult, and the child, or, abbreviated, **P**, **A**, **C**. Berne explains that the parent ego state is composed of thoughts, feelings, and ways of behaving which we copied from our parents and carry along with us throughout our lives. The material in the parent ego state tends to be quite critical and judgmental but also can be helpful and nurturing The child ego state, Berne says, is composed of the thoughts, feelings, and behaviors which we experienced as children and still retain. Material in the child ego state can be either "adapted," in other words, things others expected from us, or "natural" like joy, wonder, and excitement.

Berne describes the adult ego state as being that area where objective thought, feeling, and behavior are processed. It is the last ego state to develop, but evidence of it can be seen in very small children.[7]

Berne explains that any communication interaction can be studied using the diagram in figure 2. The diagram shows the three ego states of two people involved in an interaction. When plotting an interaction, it is necessary to try to determine from which ego state in Person 1 a comment is being made and to which ego state in Person 2 it is directed. The same process is used in trying to analyze Person 2's response.

Let's look at the example in figure 3. From the direction of the arrows, you can see that Person 1 is coming from his child ego state to Person 2's parent ego state and that

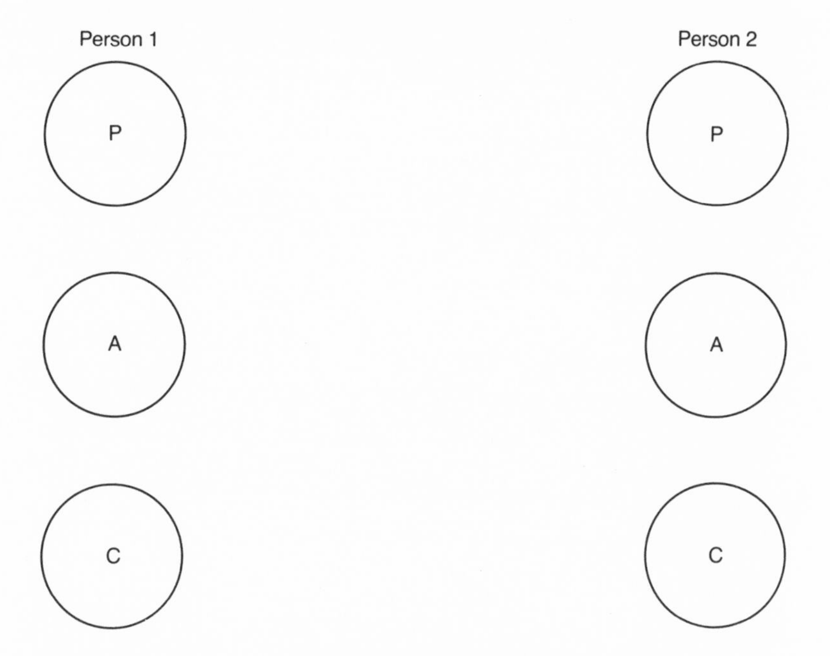

Figure 2. *Ego States*

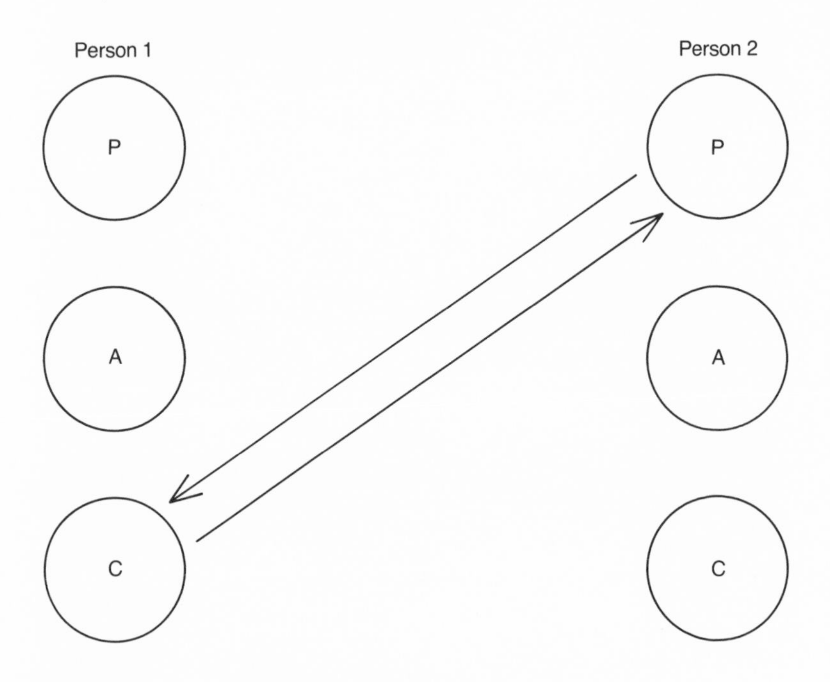

Person 1: I can't do this all by myself.
Person 2: You never really try to do anything.

Figure 3. *A Complementary Transaction*

she is responding to him as a parent would to a child, which is what he expected.

Berne calls this type of transaction *complementary.* (This should not be confused with Watzlawick, *et al.* use of the same term.) In other words, if when diagramming a transaction the lines are parallel, the transaction is complementary. If, however, the lines are not parallel, the transaction is *crossed.* Using a similar example, if Person 2 had responded to Person 1's comment, "I can't do this all by myself" with something like "I think if you turn the handles, it will fit," the diagram would look like figure 4.

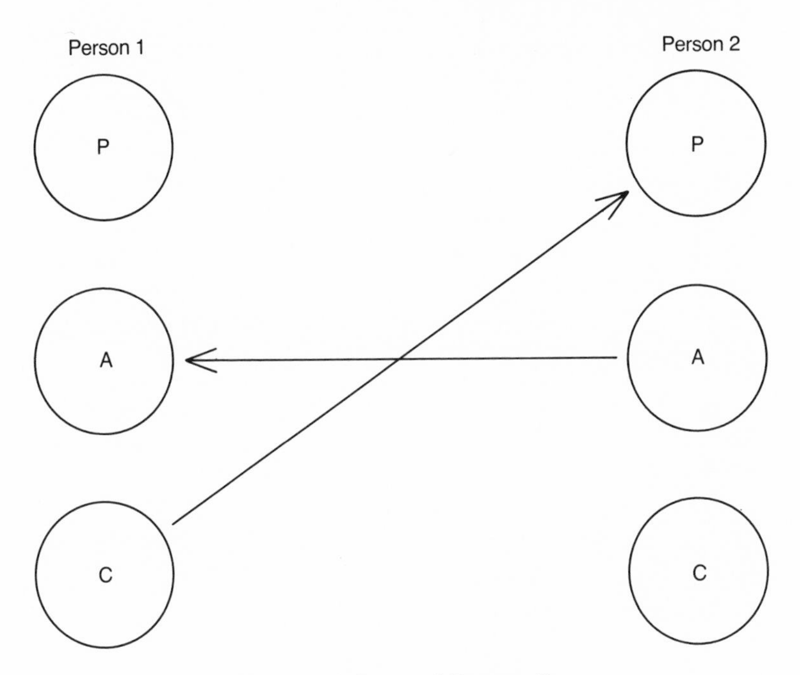

Figure 4. *A Crossed Transaction*

In this case Person 1 is still coming from his child ego state and directing his comment to Person 2's parent ego state. She, however, is responding to him as an adult would to an adult. This is a crossed transaction. When this situation occurs, Berne explains, there will be some problem in the communication system; Person 1 might be very hurt since he had not received the kind of message sought.[8]

In discussing the two types of transactions among people, Berne states the following:

> The first rule of communication is that communication will proceed smoothly as long as transactions are complementary; and its corollary is that as long as transactions are complementary, communication can, in principle, proceed indefinitely. These rules

> are independent of the nature and content of the transactions; they are based entirely on the direction of the vectors [arrows] involved.[9]

This statement is in line with our previous discussion of the possibility of looking at the effects of various messages within a communication system through an examination of the *relationship* aspects of the messages exchanged. *Regardless of the content,* Berne says, if the messages exchanged among people are complementary, communication will continue; in other words, the system will maintain itself indefinitely. Taking this idea one step further, we can see that if the messages exchanged between people result in a *crossed* transaction, some change will have to be made in the system if it is to survive. Let us look at an example of this kind of situation.

An example often used by writers discussing Berne's Transactional Analysis (popularly known at T.A.) is similar to the following:

Husband:	Do you know where my socks are?
two possible responses for *Wife:*	1: In the top drawer of the dresser.
	2: If you put things where they belong, you'd know where they are!

This transaction often has been diagrammed as in figure 5.

In both cases the husband is shown as coming from his adult and directing his comment to his wife's adult: he is simply asking for information. In the first case the wife supplies the requested information and, therefore, is responding from her adult to his adult. In the second case, however, the wife is not supplying the requested information but rather is responding to her husband very much as a parent would to a child: she is scolding him.

As diagrammed, the first transaction is complementary and the second is crossed. If transactions are crossed,

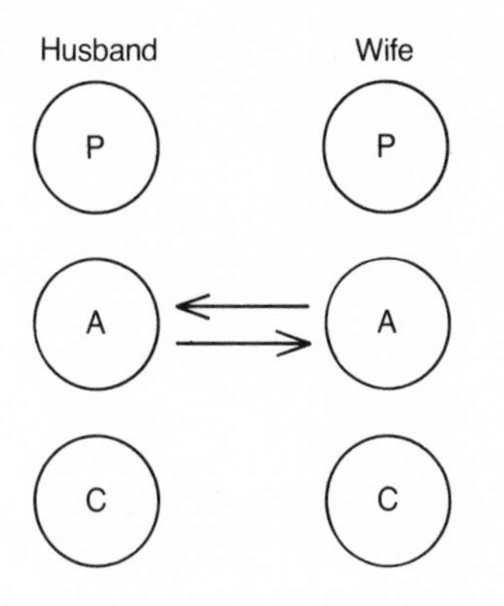

H: Do you know where my socks are?
W: In the top drawer of the dresser.

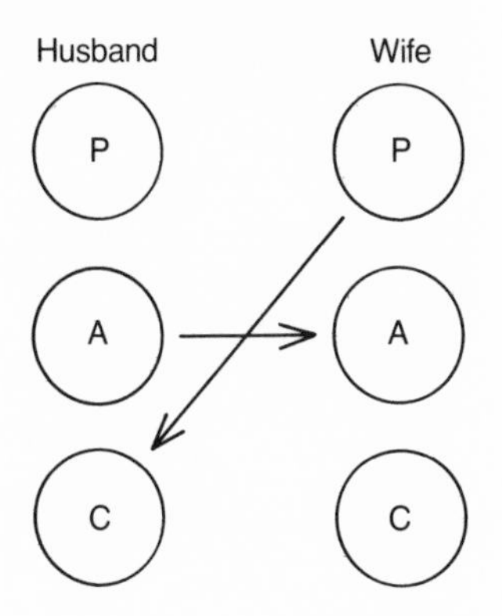

H: Do you know where my socks are?
W: If you put things where they belong, you'd know where they are!

Figure 5. *A Complementary or a Crossed Transaction?*

there will be problems in the system and something will have to change if the system is to maintain itself.

In this example, it may be necessary for the wife to try to switch to her adult in responding to her husband in similar situations. One of the problems involved, however, is the initial *assumption* which has been made that the husband is coming from his adult ego state. In this example it is entirely possible that the wife does not *perceive* the husband's comment as coming from his adult ego state (why should *she* know where his socks are!) but rather from his child to her parent. In this case the transaction could be diagrammed as in figure 6.

Now the transaction is complementary and as such the system will continue as it is. Suppose, however, that the wife is dissatisfied with the role she feels her husband is attempting to put her in. Since crossed transactions necessitate a change in a system if it is to be maintained, she may

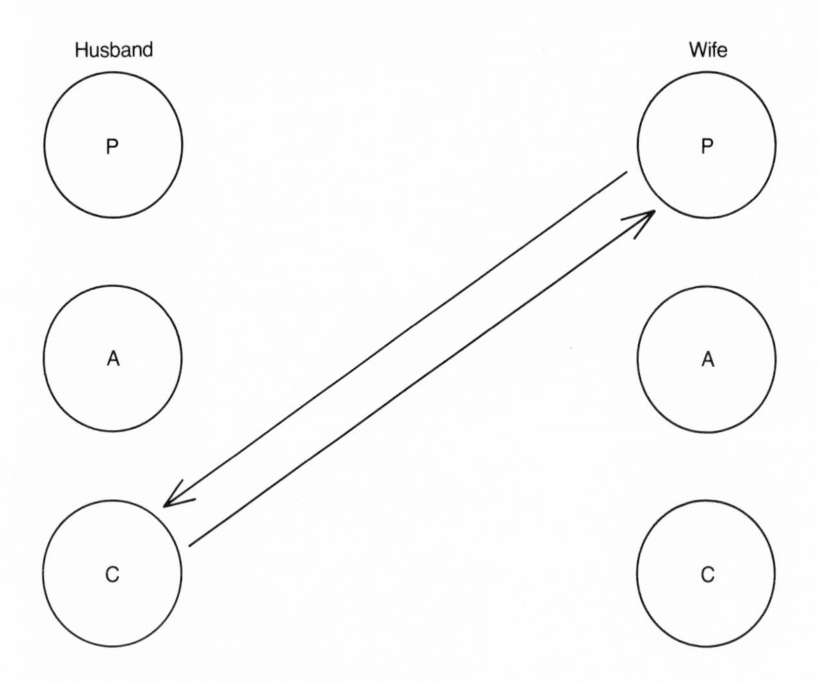

H: Do you know where my socks are?
W: If you put things where they belong, you'd know where they are!

Figure 6. *A Complementary Transaction*

elect to respond in a way which will initiate some change. An example of this is illustrated in figure 7.

In this case we can very clearly see that something within the system will have to change if it is to be maintained. This example also illustrates the importance of what we previously referred to as punctuation. In other words, in any of the above crossed transactions, the husband and wife probably would disagree over who "started" the argument which may have followed his question!

Using Berne's theories, then, we can study the messages exchanged within a communication system and de-

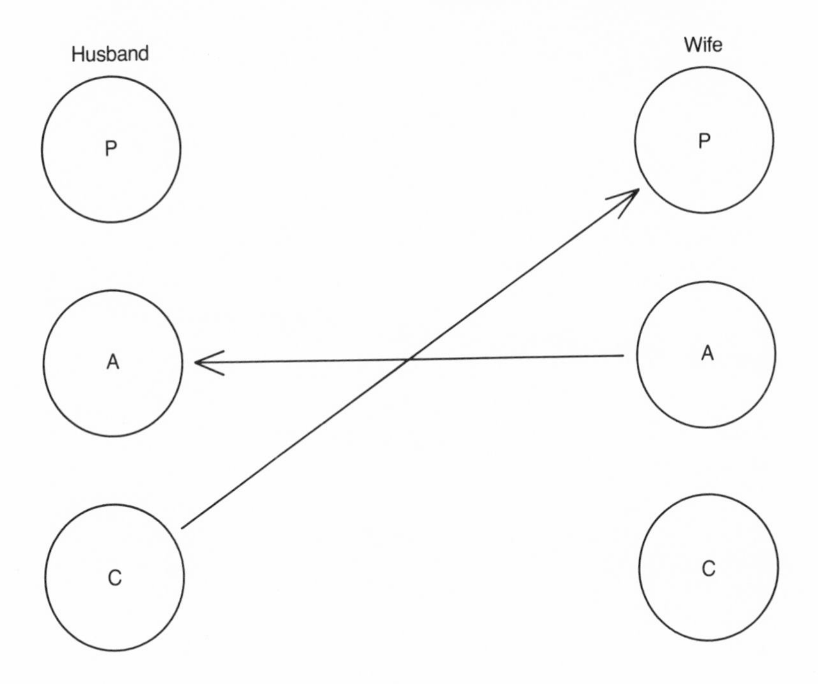

H: Do you know where my socks are?
W: You know, honey, I really get tired of your asking me things like that and I don't understand why you think *I* should know where *your* clothes are.

Figure 7. *A Crossed Transaction*

termine what the relationship aspects are by classifying the ego-state source and intended ego-state destination of each message. From these observations, we can discover patterns of messages exchanged and make predictions about how the communication system will operate.

If the messages exchanged tend to proceed in a complementary pattern, we can predict that the system will function smoothly. If there are numerous crossed transactions, we can predict that some change will have to be made, if the system is to be maintained, and we may even be able to suggest what some of those changes might be. In any case, however, how the individuals involved *perceive* what is happening is of primary importance.

Rogers

In a different way, Carl Rogers also has provided us with a method for observing the interrelationships within a communication system. As we discussed in the previous chapter, Rogers describes what he calls a facilitative or helping relationship as being one in which the people involved are helping each other to become all that they can be. As in the other theories we have discussed, the *content* aspects of the messages exchanged among the people in the system is not nearly so important as the *relationship* aspects.

In describing the kinds of messages he has found most helpful, Rogers uses such terms as *nonjudgmental, open,* and *accepting.* It is Rogers' theory that messages which convey this kind of feeling eventually elicit the same kind of messages in return. In other words, if a person's messages to another seem to indicate to him that she accepts him for what he is and that she is being open in relation to him and to herself, he in turn will come to accept himself and become more open and accepting of her.

Taking what Rogers has suggested, then, we could study the messages exchanged within a system to determine whether or not a pattern would develop along the lines he has described and, conversely, if the opposite kind of pattern occurs when the relationship components of the messages are nonaccepting, judgmental, and critical.[10]

We have presented here three of the ways in which messages within a communication system could be studied in order to understand more fully the interrelationships within the system. And when we talk about interrelationships within a communication system, we are talking about the relationships between people as manifested in the messages they exchange. We also have attempted to show that through the study of the relationship components of messages, it may be possible to discover patterns within the messages exchanged and thereby predict what will happen in the system or try to correct a system if that is what those involved in it desire.

CONCLUSION

Let us look one last time at the Transactional Model of Communication offered by Barnlund.

The study of communication involves the study of mes-

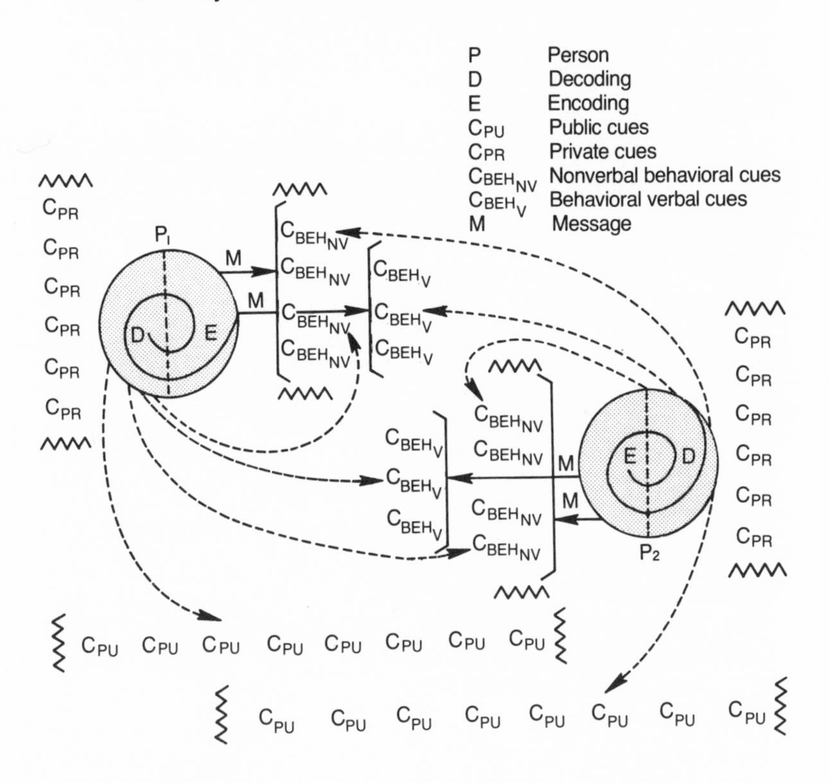

Figure 8. *The Transactional Model of Communication*

sages exchanged among people. There are many channels these messages can take, as discussed in chapter 2. In general, the messages exchanged among people can be divided into verbal ($\mathbf{C}_{BEH_V}$) and the nonverbal ($\mathbf{C}_{BEH_{NV}}$).

As can be seen from Barnlund's model, a communication system, as an open system, exists and functions within an environment, and the people involved in the system can utilize various aspects of this environment ($\mathbf{C}_{PU}$ and perhaps $\mathbf{C}_{PR}$) while functioning within the system. As the elements in the system, the people involved make up the system, and how they function within it depends entirely upon their own perceptions. These perceptions include the meanings they assign to themselves, to others, and to all aspects of the environment, in other words, the world around them.

NOTES

1. Paul Watzlawick, Janet Helmick Beavin, and Don D. Jackson, *Pragmatics of Human Communication* (New York: W. W. Norton and Co., 1967), pp. 51–54.
2. Ibid., pp. 67–70.
3. Ibid., p. 70.
4. Ibid., pp. 56–57.
5. Eric Berne, *Games People Play* (New York: Grove Press, 1964).
6. Thomas A. Harris, *I'm O.K., You're O.K.* (New York: Harper and Row, 1969).
7. Berne, pp. 23–28.
8. Ibid., pp. 29–34.
9. Ibid., p. 30.
10. Carl Rogers, *On Becoming a Person* (Boston: Houghton Mifflin Co., 1961), pp. 31–38.

BIBLIOGRAPHY

Barnlund, Dean C. "A Transactional Model of Communication." In *Language Behavior: A Book of Readings in Communication*, compiled by Johnnye Aken, Alvin Goldberg, Gail Myers, and John Stewart, pp. 43–61. The Hague: Mouton, 1970.

Bartley, S. Howard, ed. *Perception in Everyday Life.* New York: Harper and Row, 1972.

Bedichek, Roy. *The Sense of Smell.* Garden City, N.Y.: Doubleday and Co., 1960.

Bennis, Warren G.; Schein, Edkar H.; Steele, Fred I.; and Berlew, David E., eds. *Interpersonal Dynamics.* Homewood, Ill.: The Dorsey Press, 1968.

Berlo, David K. *The Process of Communication.* New York: Holt, Rinehart, and Winston, 1960.

Berne, Eric. *Games People Play.* New York: Grove Press, 1964.

Boulding, Kenneth E. *The Image.* Ann Arbor: University of Michigan Press, 1969.

Brown, Roger. *Social Psychology.* New York: The Free Press, 1965.

———. *Words and Things.* New York: The Free Press, 1958.

Cantril, Hadley. "Perception and Interpersonal Relations." *American Journal of Psychiatry* 114 (1957), 119–26.

Cooley, Charles Horton. *Human Nature and the Social Order.* New York: Charles Scribner's Sons, 1902.

Dance, Frank E. X., ed. *Human Communciation Theory.* New York: Holt, Rinehart, and Winston, 1967.

Doty, Richard I., "The Role of Olfaction in Man: Sense or Nonsense?" In *Perception in Everyday Life*, edited by S. Howard Bartley, pp. 143–157. New York: Harper and Row, 1972.

Ekman, Paul, and Friesen, Wallace V. "Head and Body Cues in the Judgment of Emotion: A Reformulation." *Perceptual and Motor Skills* 24 (1967), 711–24.

Festinger, Leon. "A Theory of Social Comparison Processes." *Human Relations* 7 (1954), 117–40.

Frank, Lawrence K. "Tactile Communication." *Genetic Psychology Monographs* 56 (1957), 209–25.

Gregory, R. L. *Eye and Brain.* New York: McGraw-Hill, 1966.

Hall, Edward T. *The Hidden Dimension.* Garden City, N.Y.: Doubleday and Co., 1966.

———. *The Silent Language.* Garden City, N.Y.: Doubleday and Co., 1959.

Harris, Thomas A. *I'm O.K., You're O.K.* New York: Harper and Row, 1969.

Harrison, Randall P. *Beyond Words: An Introduction to Nonverbal Communication.* Englewood Cliffs, N.J.: Prentice-Hall, 1974.

Hayakawa, S. I. *Language in Thought and Action.* New York: Harcourt, Brace and World, 1941.

James, William. *Psychology: The Briefer Course.* 1892. Reprint. New York: Harper and Row, 1961.

Jourard, Sidney M. *Disclosing Man to Himself.* Princeton, N.J.: D. Van Nostrand Co., 1968.

———. *The Transparent Self.* Rev. ed. New York: Van Nostrand Reinhold Co., 1971.

Kilpatrick, Franklin P., ed. *Explorations in Transactional Psychology.* New York: New York University Press, 1961.

Knapp, Mark L. *Nonverbal Communication in Human Interaction.* New York: Holt, Rinehart, and Winston, 1972.

Korzybski, Alfred. *Science and Sanity.* Lakeville, Conn.: The International Non-Aristotelian Library Publishing Co., 1933.

Luft, Joseph. *Group Processes: An Introduction to Group Dynamics.* Palo Alto, Calif.: National Press Books (now Mayfield Publishing Company), 1970.

Milne, Lorus, and Milne, Margery. *The Senses of Animals and Men.* New York: Atheneum, 1962.

Montagu, Ashley. *Touching: The Human Significance of the Skin.* New York: Harper and Row, 1971.

Ogden, C. K., and Richards, I. A. *The Meaning of Meaning.* New York: Harcourt, Brace & Co., 1923.

Rogers, Carl R. *On Becoming a Person.* Boston: Houghton Mifflin Co., 1961.

Scheflen, Albert E. "Quasi-Courtship Behavior in Psychotherapy." *Psychiatry* 28 (1965), 245–57.

———. "The Significance of Posture in Communication Systems." *Psychiatry* 27 (1964), 316–31.

Shannon, C. E., and Weaver, W. *The Mathematical Theory of Communication.* Urbana: University of Illinois Press, 1949.

Sullivan, Harry Stack. *The Interpersonal Theory of Psychiatry.* New York: W. W. Norton and Co., 1953.

Vernon, M. D. *The Psychology of Perception.* 2d ed. Baltimore: Penguin, 1971.

Watzlawick, Paul; Beavin, Janet Hilmick; and Jackson, Don D.

Pragmatics of Human Communication. New York: W. W. Norton and Co., 1967.

Wilentz, Joan Steen. *The Senses of Man.* New York: Thomas Y. Crowell Co., 1968.

FOR FURTHER READINGS

Condon, John C., and Yousef, Fathi S. *An Introduction to Intercultural Communication.* New York: The Bobbs-Merrill Co., 1975.

In this book the authors discuss many aspects of interpersonal communication as they relate specifically to situations in which people of different cultures are communicating with one another.

Gergen, Kenneth J. *The Concept of Self.* New York: Holt, Rinehart and Winston, 1971.

The author presents a brief review of the many ways self-concept has been studied in the past both theoretically and experimentally.

Goffman, Erving. *The Presentation of Self in Everyday Life.* Garden City, N.Y.: Doubleday and Co., 1959.

This book is one of the author's earliest writings which outlines his dramaturgical, descriptive approach to human interaction. He deals with both how we present ourselves to other people and how we rely upon them to uphold this presentation.

Goldberg, Alvin A., and Larson, Carl E. *Group Communication.* Englewood Cliffs, N.J.: Prentice-Hall, 1975.

Goldberg and Larson present a good introduction to the traditional concepts in the field of group dynamics with a very readable emphasis on empirical studies of group communication behavior.

Gordon, Chad, and Gergen, Kenneth J., eds. *The Self in Social Interaction.* Vol. 1. New York: John Wiley and Sons, 1968.

This book of readings contains selections from many of the researchers who have been important in the study of self as a psychological concept important to the understanding of human interaction.

Hayakawa, S. I. *Language in Thought and Action.* New York: Harcourt, Brace, & Co., 1941.

This book has remained one of the important books in the field of semantics. The abundant use of examples and "applications" which one can do while going through the book make it fun to read.

James, Muriel, and Jongeward, Dorothy. *Born to Win: Transactional Analysis with Gestalt Experiments.* Reading, Mass.: Addison-Wesley Publishing Co., 1971.

This book reflects the growing popularity of Eric Berne's Transactional Analysis (TA) by providing a very readable description of the foundations of TA and many instructive exercises for the reader to perform.

Laing, R. D.; Phillipson, H.; and Lee, A. R. *Interpersonal Perception.* New York: Harper and Row, 1966.

In this book Laing describes the process of spiraling interpersonal perceptions which was ultimately illustrated in his book *Knots* and presents a way of untangling the knots we create by use of the Interpersonal Perception Method (IPM).

Maslow, Abraham H. *Toward a Psychology of Being.* New York: Van Nostrand Reinhold Co., 1968.

In this book the author, one of the forces in the development of humanistic psychology, presents his views of the possibilities of human growth through various "levels" and, finally, approach to real self-actualization.

Perls, Frederick; Hefferline, Ralph E., and Goodman, Paul. *Gestalt Therapy.* New York: Dell Publishing Co., 1951.

In this book the authors present the underlying framework of Gestalt therapy and include many exercises for the reader to perform while learning the theoretical foundations of Perl's approach.

Postman, Neil; Weingartner, Charles; and Moran, Terence P., eds. *Language in America.* New York: Western Publishing Co., 1969.

As the authors state in the introduction, "This book is intended to serve as a check on some of the many 'languages' currently being used in America to codify reality." (p. ix). Some of the languages included are the Language of Politics, of Bureaucracy, of Censorship, of Racism, of Advertising, of Education, and so on, each one described by a writer in a position to know what (s)he is talking about.

Scheflen, Albert, and Scheflen, Alice. *Body Language and Social Order.* Englewood Cliffs, N. J.: Prentice-Hall, 1972.

In this book the authors present the primary aspects of Scheflen's contextual-analysis approach to studying nonverbal communication. The discussion is well illustrated with pictures throughout which help greatly in understanding the approach.

Tagiuri, Renato, and Petrullo, Luigi, eds. *Person Perception and Interpersonal Behavior.* Stanford, Calif.: Stanford University Press, 1958.

This book contains writings from many different authors all of which focus in some way on the process of people perceiving other people and how these perceptions influence interpersonal behavior.

INDEX